KIND
FOLKS
FINISH
FIRST

KIND FOLKS FINISH FIRST

THE **CONSIDERATE PATH** TO **SUCCESS** IN **BUSINESS** AND **LIFE**

SAM JACOBS
WITH **KERRI LINSENBIGLER**

WILEY

Published by John Wiley & Sons, Inc., Hoboken, New Jersey.
Published simultaneously in Canada.

For general information on our other products and services or for technical support, please contact our Customer Care Department within the United States at (800) 762-2974, outside the United States at (317) 572-3993 or fax (317) 572-4002.

Wiley also publishes its books in a variety of electronic formats. Some content that appears in print may not be available in electronic formats. For more information about Wiley products, visit our web site at www.wiley.com.

Library of Congress Cataloging-in-Publication Data

Names: Jacobs, Sam (Chief Executive Officer), author.
Title: Kind folks finish first : the considerate path to success in
   business and life / Sam Jacobs.
Description: Hoboken, New Jersey : Wiley, [2023] I Includes index.
Identifiers: LCCN 2022035660 (print) I LCCN 2022035661 (ebook) I ISBN
   9781119983002 (hardback) I ISBN 9781119983026 (adobe pdf) I ISBN
   9781119983019 (epub)
Subjects: LCSH: Success in business. I Kindness.
Classification: LCC HF5386 .J3123 2023 (print) I LCC HF5386 (ebook) I DDC
   650.1—dc23/eng/20220907
LC record available at https://lccn.loc.gov/2022035660
LC ebook record available at https://lccn.loc.gov/2022035661

Cover Design: Wiley
Cover Image: © Julia August/Getty Images

SKY10036128_092122

For those who believe in a better way to do business.

CONTENTS

ACKNOWLEDGMENTS

There are too many people to properly thank for the community we've all built together over the past eight years. But a few that come to mind include Fred Mather, one of our earliest and most vocal supporters, Anne Juceam, our very first full-time employee, and all the original Members of the New York Revenue Collective.

We wouldn't be here without the support of Max Altschuler, Founder and CEO of Sales Hacker, who launched the podcast with me and who introduced me to Wiley in the first place.

The first seven Chapter Heads played a critical role in our growth including Tom Glason, Rich Gardner, Butch Langlois, André Bressel, Kyle Lacy, Nicole Smith, and Joshua Amrani.

None of this would have happened without the support of my wife, Camille, who has stuck with me through thick and thin from my penniless days post-Axial to today over close to 13 amazing years and helped bring so many beautiful animals into our lives, especially my beloved Walter.

Thanks also to my amazing family, including my mom, Ambassador Susan Jacobs, my dad, Barry Jacobs, my brother and sister, Josh and Wendy, my nieces and nephews, and especially Buster.

Special thanks to Kerri Linsenbigler for helping me finish the book, to Jared Rosen for being our first book coach, and the entire team at Wiley, including Shannon Vargo, Sally Baker, and Julie Kerr for their support.

And, of course, thanks to our thousands and thousands of Members who live our values every day and, in so doing, help demonstrate that kind folks really can finish first.

INTRODUCTION:
THE STORY OF PAVILION

There is a fallacy in the business world that to succeed you have to be ruthless. There is one way to get rich and have truly global impact and that is to screw the other person before they screw you. Lots of people have succeeded based on that philosophy.

I'm here to tell you there is a different way. Being a jerk, focusing on the short term, emphasizing "the art of the deal" above long-term relationships—perhaps that is one path.

But within the world, there are many paths to success. The path I will lay out for you offers the same things—wealth, impact, a legacy. But it does so in a way that will make you feel good. That will put positive energy into the universe. That will uplift you and those around you.

And to begin your journey, you don't need a wild stroke of luck. You don't need a trust fund. And you don't need to be a perennially upbeat happy person oblivious to the reality of the world around you. In fact, I'm pretty much the opposite of that. I'm grumpy. I'm moody.

But the lessons I articulate in this book are about a deeper sense of compassion and kindness. They are not about your mood. They are about a way of behaving in the world. A way that aligns you with positivity.

Some of it may seem hokey. And some of it may seem naive. There's a certain power and sense of superiority in cynicism. That's certainly true. It's up to you how you choose to lead your life. And this is just one way. But it's a way that I've found to work.

If you take that leap with me and go with me on this journey, I'm confident you'll come out on the other side with a deeper connection to success. We'll work through some of the challenges and objections you might naturally raise, and I'll share with you deeply personal information about my decades-long struggles with the right sense of self, with depression, and with my near perpetual frustration with my station and place in life and with my career.

But, on the other side of all of that, you'll also discover what I've learned to truly change my life. To finally discover happiness. To build the tools I use almost every day to nurture that happiness. And to work through how that happiness and peace has transcended my professional life and impacted my life at home with my wife and my personal relationships.

This is a book about the company I started now called Pavilion, originally called Revenue Collective. I did not intend to start a big company. I only intended to help my friends find jobs and to create a group of people committed to supporting each other. But somehow, years later that company is worth more than $200 million and doubling while barely burning any capital.

This is also a book about how I saved my marriage, discovered true happiness for the first time in my life, and achieved almost everything I'd dreamed, and more, since I started working back in 1999.

Prior to starting Pavilion, I'd been a vice president of sales at venture-capital backed companies in New York City beginning in 2003 when I started at Gerson Lehrman Group. I'd risen up through the ranks quickly at GLG, which became a big company while I was there.

I left in 2010 to set out on my journey of becoming a C-level executive. I'd always harbored big dreams and ambitions, but the next eight years were a series of false starts and frustrations that created a terrifying sense of repetition. That I wasn't making actual progress. That I wouldn't become wealthy and that I wouldn't realize the sense of potential I felt inside myself and have felt since I was a young child.

Beginning in 2014, I started bringing my friends together for dinner every quarter in New York. These were other people in similar situations. People in their thirties and forties working at high-growth companies and struggling to see the light at the end of the rainbow, struggling to see how all the toil and hard work would ultimately end in some kind of big payday, some kind of recognition.

So we started having dinner together every quarter. Then we started emailing each other with questions about work, how we had approached different challenges and obstacles, how we'd solved different problems. What email subject lines were working. What the ratio of salespeople to sales managers was and how to motivate and retain great talent and develop them.

These were all questions that were too real and too recent to have studied in a book and the book would have been out of date if it had offered answers anyway.

From those email threads and those dinners, something began to emerge and take hold. Now, a dinner club is not the hardest thing in the world to copy. And an email distribution is not a hard thing to copy either.

I never thought what we were doing could be a big business because I thought, "There must be a sales executive meetup in every city in the world. I don't know why there doesn't seem to be one in New York, but New York is a big place and I'll just do the one in New York."

My thought process was intentionally modest. I didn't give myself permission to think what I was working on was a venture-scale business—something that could become a unicorn or decacorn or change thousands or tens of thousands or hundreds of thousands of people's lives. I just thought I enjoyed helping people. It gave me a sense of purpose and accomplishment. It filled me up with a sense of satisfaction.

In fact, when I first left my last full-time job to work on Pavilion full-time in December of 2018, I only hoped I could get it to 2,000 paying Members.

Now, I'm writing these words in 2022. What started off as a dinner club in New York with me and a few of my friends has become a global community of over 10,000. In April of 2021, just a few years after launching, we received a $25 million investment from Elephant Ventures, valuing the company at north of $100 million and we've grown threefold since that investment. Not only that, but in the course of that investment, I was able to sell some of my ownership in Pavilion and achieve actual wealth—a goal that had seemed forever beyond my grasp as I came of age in New York beginning in 2003.

This book is that story of the change in me that occurred over the past five years, beginning in 2017. A change that proved transformational and helped me build a global company at scale, impact the lives of thousands, and achieve nearly all of my professional goals.

I had sensed the possibilities of the ideas espoused in this book for a long time. In fact, I'd practiced them subconsciously and unintentionally. But it was beginning in 2017 that I was finally able to start getting a sense of how to put these principles into some kind of framework.

I often joke that so many business books are really just articles turned into books to convey gravity or spurious sincerity. And perhaps I'm guilty of that over the next 200 pages. But the framework is indeed simple and straightforward.

That framework is also not new. It's been promulgated by everyone from Oprah to Tony Robbins to Adam Grant to Dan Pink and on and on.

Condensed into its essence it is simple and straightforward:

Look to help others before you help yourself. Do as much as you can for other people and ask nothing in return. Try as hard as you can to stop keeping score. Play a long big game instead of a short small game. Build relationships not transactions. And try to use the power of love, optimism, and gratitude to power as much of your decision making as possible.

It's that simple. It's not easy. But it's simple.

The point of the book is that doing these things—embracing kindness, consideration, reciprocity, and a sense of spirituality powered by love is not just something you do because it makes you feel good. Of course, it does make you feel good.

But these are practices you can embrace not just to feel good but to achieve the things you want to achieve in your professional life. You can use these practices to get rich and make a lot of money. You can use these practices to get a promotion. You can use these practices to rise to the top of your profession.

There is an old adage: Nice guys finish last.

That adage is wrong. It's wrong not just because it conjures up some notion that "guys" are the only people that participate in business. Of course that's false. But it's wrong too because at its essence it implies that business is zero-sum, that the only way for you to win is for someone else to lose. That the world is implicitly dog eat dog.

I don't believe that, and in the times when I have believed that nothing has gone right for me.

My life changed when I realized that the beauty of regulated capitalism is that in order to achieve the things you want you have to build things other people want. At its essence, it is a deeply humane system and the most efficient allocator of resources in human history. (Side note: Let's make sure we emphasize I am using the word "regulated." I am aware that unfettered capitalism has inherent flaws baked into it. But that's a story for another book.)

My life changed when I realized that helping other people without asking for anything in return, that playing a game so long I didn't have to keep track of it, that helping for helping's sake, was itself a competitive advantage. Because so few people do it. So few people truly practice it and embrace these ideas and these philosophies. So when you do, you stand out. You look different.

My life changed when I realized that the universe is far more malleable than we realize. That thoughts become actions. And that the underlying power driving all of it is or can be love and generosity.

That's what this book is about. That's what these subsequent chapters are about.

The journey of building a company now worth over $200 million and doing it in a profitable sustainable way. The principles that led me here. And the simple easy practices you can implement in your life that can transform not just how you feel and approach your professional life but that can actually help you achieve your goals.

The book begins by reframing your perspective on yourself and your life, and resolving to change. That's Chapter 1. From there, we dive into some tools you can use to discover your true passion and to align your passion and your skills with possibilities for success. Because this is also the story of building a company, we'll layer in some practical business concepts that can help you if you're running your own company or working on someone else's. And finally, we'll go deep on the underlying principles that can transform the foundation you've laid. Those principles are fundamentally rooted in spirituality. And that spirituality is fundamentally powered by love. By a sense of gratitude and appreciation. And that, through love, compassion, gratitude, and appreciation, you can work to manifest the world you want to live in. One where kindness is rewarded. Where love and openness creates the possibility of transformation. And maybe, just maybe, a world that you can get the things you most desire.

I hope you enjoy it.

Chapter 1

Fired at the Rest Stop

THE POWER OF FAILURE

"I'm about to get fired again."

I was on the New Jersey Turnpike, a long industrial stretch of road connecting cloverleaves in Delaware to my home in New York City. Along the way are rest stops named after people you've sort of heard of. Clara Barton. Vince Lombardi. Richard Fenwick.

My wife, my dog, and I pulled over at the Richard Fenwick Rest Area. I'd just received one of those emails that puts a pit in your stomach. My wife Camille watched me scroll through the email in dead silence. After an eternal minute I glanced up with a deadened look in my eyes. She waited patiently, but quizzically.

It was Friday the 13th, October 2017.

My track record as a startup executive was discouraging. I'd now worked at four companies over the past 14 years and this would be the third time I was fired. My self-esteem plummeted as I read the message. How fitting to be at a rest stop when my career was in the toilet. Again.

"I'm about to get fired again."

I thought back on the 18 years since I graduated from the University of Virginia—failure seemed to be a constant theme.

I'd started a record label, moved to a farm in rural Virginia, and tried to become some kind of hipster media mogul. That didn't work.

I'd followed a girl back to New York. We got married. Then the marriage fell apart.

I somehow found myself in the world of high-tech venture capital–backed startups. I'd thought getting into the

11

C-suite and working hand-in-hand with the CEO might translate to job security. What an oxymoron.

"I'm about to get fired again."

What was the root of all my failures? I worked for incredibly successful companies, filled with incredibly smart, talented people. Yet, I was left with a sickness inside myself that created a sense of transactional competition and insecurity that I tried to cover up with the money I was making.

"I'm about to get fired again."

On the New Jersey Turnpike, the email itself was seemingly innocuous. A note from my CEO saying "I hadn't realized you'd be out today. Can we meet first thing Monday morning?"

She wasn't a morning person.

"I'm about to get fired again."

I was at an inflection point. My adult life up to this point was marred by struggle and dissatisfaction. I never felt I could get my feet under me. I never felt I was doing what I was meant to do. I always felt I was at someone else's whim.

There and then, in that rest stop parking lot, I resolved that this firing would be different. I can't quite describe the resolve I had. The determination that suddenly formed inside of me. But I had a certainty. A certainty that this was going to be the last time this type of situation happened to me. I wasn't going to wallow. I wasn't going to feel sorry for myself. I was sick of letting life happen to me.

I was going to take control and use this moment to transform. To rise above the chop and the froth and the turbulence that kept upending my life and find a new path forward. To catapult myself into the life I wanted to live. I was going to leap into the unknown and simply trust that I'd figure it out. Figure out how to support myself on my own terms. And figure out how to finally achieve true independence.

GETTING FIRED STILL SUCKS

Despite this parking lot revelation, getting fired sucks. That's obvious, and yet still surprising to so many of us.

As a child, I always viewed myself with nearly limitless potential. I had been good at school and gotten good grades. I got where I wanted to go.

The first time I was fired was back in 2010. I was sitting in an office discussing leaving Gerson Lehrman Group, realizing this wasn't really a choice, but an order. I was getting fired—and I was stunned.

The truth was that I was treated well in my departure from GLG. Alexander Saint-Amand, the CEO at the time, was honest and direct while still being caring. He told me as much as he wanted me to stay at the company, there wasn't a department head that wanted me on their team. I was too surly. Too disgruntled. Always complaining. So there was literally nothing much he could do, and he was right. I had pushed myself out of the company somehow.

Each time you get fired you can lose a little piece of yourself if you're not careful. Even if you use the firing to reframe the next chapter of your life, it still sucks.

The second time I got fired was not as nice.

When I was asked to leave GLG, I found myself at another startup, with a big pay cut and in the throes of a divorce.

I worked there a long time and built it from nothing into something. Me and a bunch of other folks. But I was disgruntled again. Thinking I had contributed too much and controlled too little. And I'd lost respect for the CEO. So I tried to get him fired. I secretly met with an investor and shared my frustration. They said they'd look into it and then followed up to let me know they didn't think it was a good idea and they were going to stick with the current leader. Months went by.

So much time had passed, I thought I was in the clear. I thought I'd somehow avoided discovery. I even got promoted to Senior Vice President. I'd been at the company for four and a half years at that point and had an inflated sense of my own importance to the company and my job security. There's that oxymoron again.

Then one day, the CEO and I went for one of our typical Monday walks, but there was a notable difference in his tone of voice. About halfway through, I realized I was getting fired. And this time it was not a graceful exit, but the kind where they turn off your email and lock you out of every system and then tell you that you can't go back to the office and please return the laptop. The most embarrassing and painful way to get fired. I had a team of close to 60 but wasn't permitted to say goodbye to any of them, many of whom I'd personally hired and developed and who I thought of almost as family. I still remember the head of HR, a very nice person and still the best marathon coach I've ever had, meeting me at the Grey Dog Cafe so that I could give back the company laptop. It's hard to put into words the level of shame and embarrassment I felt. A deep darkness came over me back then and lodged itself somewhere in my psyche.

That time I did wallow. I smoked a joint and drove out to Jones Beach to look at the Venetian tower and lie on the sand and listen to "Let It Bleed" by the Rolling Stones. Trying to figure out where to go from there. And how to pick myself back up.

Those painful experiences prepared me for the signals I needed to look out for when I got fired from The Muse two jobs later. The shift in tone. The abrupt meeting. The "pack your shit and go" vibe.

So before we dive too deep into all the self-help talk about how all this is just fuel for the fire and, in hindsight, how lucky you are to have all these terrible things happen to you, let's just acknowledge that it's a deeply shitty experience.

And if it has happened to you, I want you to know that you're not alone. And it doesn't mean you're a failure. In fact, getting fired is both a deeply educational experience and one you can draw on in future years. And it's much more common than you think.

We've run numerous studies within the Pavilion Executive community evaluating how long most startup executives last in their role. We looked at various social media profiles and worked to ascertain how long each person held their position. The results were astounding. In fact, most startup executives last less than 18 months in their job, and that number has been steadily shrinking over the previous years, particularly during the COVID pandemic.

Various other companies have supported the data with Gong, the well-known revenue intelligence and call-recording company, revealing a study showing that vice presidents of sales at startups last just 19 months.

This information is a big deal. It means there is far less stability than there ever has been. Greater opportunity for sure. But far less stability. I remember growing up and hearing about people who worked on the assembly line at the Ford Motor Company. There was a pension and a clear retirement plan. They even gave you a gold watch after 20 years. You'd start working right out of college or even high school, put in your two decades, and be in a position to think about what came next in your forties and fifties.

All that is gone now. People are changing jobs more than ever before, and the reality is that, particularly in the world of fast-growth startups, and especially in sales and marketing, every day you set foot in the office or log onto a Zoom call, you are taking on great risk.

There are a variety of factors why. There's so much capital out there, and the pressure is high for every company to become the next unicorn, the next multibillion-dollar valuation. Startups go through phases of growth faster than normal companies by design, so your skills might be relevant for one stage and not another.

And as we've seen from the COVID pandemic, people's tolerances for working in inflexible, overworked, unappreciated environments are low. So maybe our own patience wears thin quicker.

But again, none of those realities matter in the moment when you realize you're about to be fired. You just feel loss and shame and anger. But, if you're like me, you will learn to understand these feelings. You will learn that these feelings are temporary, and you will grow from these setbacks. You really will. I promise.

You can use this experience to emerge better, stronger, and more powerful. Throughout this book, I'll show you how I did it.

In fact, you may just end up where I am, with gratitude. Gratitude for all the people that fired me. Gratitude for the lessons they tried to share with me that I was too stubborn to hear. Gratitude that every single experience and failure led me here, to a place where I can truly enjoy my life and where I'm still relatively young enough to do so.

THE LESSONS OF FAILURE

Failure had been such a constant presence in my adult life that it was worth breaking down some of the root causes. Something about my moment at the rest stop triggered a breakthrough for me. But why? What was it about?

I imagine if you're reading this, you can identify with this feeling of failure. This feeling of not living up to your potential. That something inside of you was trapped. And the frustration that things aren't turning out the way they were supposed to.

I've been there so many times. Pivotal inflection points in my life that were seared into my brain as representations of missed opportunity and unrealized potential. It started when I didn't get into Thomas Jefferson, the magnet school in Fairfax County, Virginia, for the best and brightest. Then, I didn't get into Princeton. I remember the thin envelope sitting in the mailbox and the breakdown it triggered. The feeling of being passed up. Passed over.

That feeling followed me to one of my bigger failures, my record label. What were the lessons? What were the reasons?

Failure of Pride

I failed at the record label because I had no idea what I was doing.

There were so many ill-fated decisions, made from pride and ego. I thought I knew it all. I leapt from investment banking into the music industry with no contacts, no network, and no experience in the industry.

I'd had friends who were musicians. It was 1999. The dot-com boom. Everyone was starting something. I'd start a record label. I'd help my friends become famous. We'd all live on a farm outside of Charlottesville, and we'd build a recording studio in the basement, and we'd make great records like the guys from the Elephant Six collective where Neutral Milk Hotel came from or Merge Records from North Carolina or the two legendary indie labels, Sub Pop, where Nirvana was first born, and Matador, home to Pavement, perhaps the greatest indie rock band of all time that stayed indie (this is a much longer discussion obviously and depends whether you think REM was an indie band, they certainly were at the beginning).

I had all these dreams of going back to Charlottesville and trying to reclaim some of the magic that was my last semester at the University of Virginia, perhaps the last time before these past few years when I was truly happy and care-free, and felt light and content.

What was really happening was some kind of wish fulfillment. Let's call it stubborn youth. Stomping my feet and saying I was going to be good at something because I said I would be.

Of course, the world said otherwise. The bands I picked to support were not very good. I wasn't as savvy with artist agreements, and, of course, I had no network to rely on to prop me up or support the work we were doing. I moved to Charlottesville but was too shy and nervous to approach the team from the Dave Matthews Band, Red Light Management, the biggest and most important music company in the area.

Instead, I rented an office, took bong hits in the basement of the farmhouse we had all rented, and subsisted on the leftover bagels the bassist would bring back from his job at Bodo's. We invented the "bagel salad sandwich"—a bagel with a bagel in the middle. We were dirt broke. Absolutely broke.

So broke that there were multiple times days before rent was due I had no idea where the money was going to come from. I took a job delivering Domino's and still remember the day I delivered a pizza to a kid skipping school. The total bill was $7.42. He gave me $7.50 and told me to keep the change. A professional low point.

I remember being alone and lonely. I remember being sad. So incredibly sad. Driving back on Route 64 from Charlottesville out to our farmhouse at 6:00 in the morning, bright sunlight, after staying up all night for no reason and listening to the song "Remember" by Air in my Volkswagen Jetta and feeling like there was a bowling ball on my chest. Like I couldn't even imagine what happiness was.

I call those years "the bad old days" for good reason.

But I did learn something. And that thing was work ethic and humility.

In fact, as I sat in the car years later at the Richard Fenwick Rest Area, I realized that in every failure I had taken away a kernel of something with me. That even though I had failed and failed again, I had made some kind of deposit in my ultimate character.

The record label taught me that pride and ego are not the requisite inputs for success. They were actually active blockers.

As you think about your life, your career, and your success, remember that nothing is owed to any of us. So much of what we get, we work for. And I don't mean through a nose-to-the-grindstone, get-there-early, leave-late type of hard work.

It's about working with humility. A sense of service. The world has much to offer us, and if we listen, we may learn from it.

Failure of Physics

Of course, sometimes the reality is that failure or the perception of failure is because of factors that are simply outside of your control in the first place. "Doing what you love" is not good advice because it ignores some obvious realities about the world. That's why we need a good perspective on the external realities that power success.

Let's dive into them, and let's think about a framework for evaluating potential paths to success.

I often tell people, "You can't outthink gravity." What I mean when I say that is that there are certain fundamental realities and principles of the universe that persist no matter what. They are the rules. That's what physics is. The rules and principles that govern reality.

When thinking about my career, an old friend once pointed out a useful heuristic. There are three key elements to success: The first is what you're good at, the second is what you're interested in doing, and the third is where the market is moving.

Most people overweight what they're interested in and underweight the market and their skills. In fact, most people don't quite understand how what they want to do translates into professional activities in the first place.

I had wanted to start a record label. Largely because I love music and fell in love with the romantic idea of living on a commune with a recording studio in the basement writing and recording music. That's my passion and my interest. But that doesn't mean there's a market there, and it doesn't necessarily mean I was in a position to run a record label in the first place, even if the market for music was growing, which, in 1999, with the launch of Napster and MP3.com, it most certainly was not.

Misclassifying What You Love

Most people, for reasons that are often cultural and disconnected from the daily activities they perform in a job, misclassify their interests. They do this because they fail to break down the actual daily activities of a job and instead ascribe blanket euphemisms to entire functions.

People say, "I don't like sales." Well, working in sales is a lot of different things. Saying it that way undercuts the possibilities.

Sales is about having conversations. Being interested and curious about other people.

It's also about competition and keeping score. About knowing exactly how you're doing. Outcomes and results. Sales is about repetition, consistency, and discipline.

So if none of those things are interesting to you, then yes, maybe you don't like sales. But perhaps you're not deeply considering the activities and the mindset that different functions require.

Outside of the record label, I've also started a number of bands myself. I learned how to write songs and found musicians who could play them better than I could. I released a few different albums under the name Lipstik and The Flying Change. I worked with my friend and producer, Paul Brill, who I'd managed during the label days. There's nothing like the thrill of having a simple melody and chord progression in your head and then months or even years later hearing that song recorded beautifully. That feeling of creation is at the core of my being. It's when I feel alive. When I, feel most human. There's nothing like it.

I still get to feel that joy of creation almost daily. And yet, I'm not in a band now.

Years later, building and running my own company, I found the same creation in activities as mundane as putting an HTML email together in Hubspot. Or coming up with a good idea and working with a team to execute.

The beauty of creation isn't exclusive to art, but can be found in all manner of activities in your life. So I would encourage you to think deeply about functions and industries that might not appear relevant on the surface, but might actually hold the promise of fulfillment within.

The Power of the Market

Perhaps one of the most critical factors driving professional success—and the thing that will paper over numerous other errors—is the market itself.

In many ways, the market is simply a proxy for the broader energy of the universe. The movement and flow of that energy propels great people, companies, and products along. If you can ride that wave, you can achieve success, often in spite of many other shortcomings.

The market is gravity. The market is physics.

The market is greater than all of us. It is the sum total of people's desires and wishes, and it determines, more than anything else, the success or failure of an endeavor. The market is everyone. The market is the universe. And to have a successful career, you can't fight the universe. You need to flow with the universe.

Now when we say a large market, typically we mean a large total number of potential customers. Of course, the most important factor is the number of total potential customers multiplied by the average amount each customer might pay. That tells you the total dollar opportunity available to you.

But a large number of potential customers is still the best way to get a big market for a bunch of pretty simple straightforward reasons. Perhaps the biggest reason of all is that you can experiment in a big market and still have an opportunity to succeed. In a small market, you might get a few things wrong and have exhausted all of your potential customer conversations before you even begin to discover your product, how to price it, or what you really want to sell. A large market creates a margin for error that lets you iterate. A large market gives you the chance to test and innovate and still have lots and lots of people to sell to.

And as you think about learning from failure and perhaps avoiding it in the future, think first and foremost about the markets in which you will operate. Because they have physics to them that you won't be able to outthink.

When you have product market fit, when you are swimming with the current, everything feels simpler, everything feels easy. I spent 7.5 years at a company called Gerson Lehrman Group selling information to investors that desperately needed that information. That company grew tenfold in the years that I was there, and I wasn't smarter or wiser than I am today. But because we had a product that people wanted and would pay for, all of our best ideas took hold.

And, thinking again of physics, many of the companies that I worked for later, did not have that same wonderful lift of the market pushing things along. When you don't have the winds of the market in your sails, everything is harder, everything becomes more desperate.

I spent 4.5 years selling leads to private equity investors that didn't have a lot of money, weren't particularly interested in paying for leads, and the leads we had to sell were the ones nobody wanted in the first place. The market itself was fairly small. There just aren't that many private equity firms out there that are operating effectively. And because we had a product that wasn't very good, we couldn't charge very much for it. And those realities are simple physics.

I realized thinking through some of the failures I'd experienced at all sorts of different companies, failures that manifested themselves as firings, so much of what I ascribed to my personal situation was simply the market.

We don't always realize that we are part of the economy, part of the broader global universal movement of energy. But we very much are.

Warren Buffett famously said, "When a management with a reputation for brilliance tackles a business with a reputation for bad economics, it is the reputation of the business that remains intact."

Buffett is talking about physics. There are forces of failure that are in your control. And there are forces of failure that are out of your control. Assuming that failure is always personal can be a grievous mistake. The agency you have in that failure is one of market selection. Of companies with "bad economics" as the Oracle of Omaha would put it.

The trick is learning that simple fact. Learning how to analyze opportunity in the right way and understand the basic, fundamental physics of a market and consequently of the universe.

I started a record label from a farm in the middle of Virginia with no network and mediocre bands. And yes that was dumb.

But more importantly, I started a record label in 1999 when the Internet was emerging, when Napster was taking hold, and when kids in college began buying computers with CD burners in them.

I started a record label in 1999 when the way record labels work is that you put down tons of money up front for recording, manufacturing, and distribution, and, if you ever get paid back at all, you get paid back years from when you invested. We call those capital-intensive businesses.

Physics.

Even if I'd had the best bands in the world, in the heart of New York City, I was entering a period of secular decline in recorded music revenue that would last for decades before artists and creators finally reset their economics and found a way to integrate streaming, merchandise, and live performance. And even then, a record label is still not the right way to capitalize on all of that.

Physics.

Failure of Mindset

But, there is something more important. The most important thing of all. And this is bigger than experience, bigger than humility, and bigger than physics even.

The biggest failure I realized as I sat in the car in 2017, was not about a lack of experience or knowledge or being in the music industry at the wrong time, or the live-streaming industry, or any industry in particular.

The diamond created from those years of repeated setbacks was formed from the realization that my biggest failure had been one of mindset.

Something had taken hold of me over the last years that was now ready to be shed, like a snake finding new skin.

That old skin had a mindset of lack, of deficiency, of wanting but not having. I had been filled with a sense of frustration at who I was and what I'd become. And I'd been caught in a trap of thinking that this frustration itself was motivating. That by being extremely dissatisfied and constantly telling myself what I didn't have, that the things I wanted would magically appear. And even more importantly, that all of success lay in money but that I didn't have the right or the ability to set off on my own, particularly after the failure of the record label so many years before.

Because of that mindset, I'd been caught in a loop for what was approaching 15 years. The key elements of the early part of my career were a company that was incredibly successful, peopled with incredibly smart talented people, but that left me with a sickness inside myself that created a sense of transactional competition, insecurity, and the idea that money itself was the input to my happiness versus the output of my happiness.

If nothing else, my hope for you, dear reader, is that you don't suffer the same fate that I did. Namely, years and years of unhappiness under the mistaken assumption that unhappiness itself led to happiness.

In fact, the truth, for me at least, was the exact opposite. The thing that ultimately created my success was not an emphasis on what I didn't have. It was the joy of what I did have. It was the release in needing other people's approval and opinions. And it was the letting go of self-pity and even the sense that I was a failure in the first place.

My entire epiphany did not happen in the rented Chevy Malibu at the Rest Stop. But what did happen was the beginning of that realization.

The Definition of Insanity

They say the definition of insanity is doing the same thing over and over again and expecting different results. And at the core of that moment in the rest stop was the emergence of a resolve to try things differently.

For years, I'd told myself that I was a failure. And that even though I was working for people I didn't always respect, I didn't have what it took to be a founder and CEO myself. Because I didn't know how to code, I couldn't build a software business as the founder. And if I couldn't build a software business, then every business by definition was a lifestyle business and not worth very much.

But sitting there at that rest stop, I had reached a breaking point of sorts. I knew that I just couldn't do it anymore and that whatever my fears were about the future, I needed to try something different.

No matter what happened, I needed to find a way to build something of my own. Something that wasn't subject to the whims and vicissitudes of founders and investors that often didn't have a clue as to what was really happening in the business. Something that emerged from the best parts of me. The parts that loved to give and to help and to serve, even if there wasn't a ton of money in it. Something that felt true.

If you've ever been pushed to the breaking point, if you feel like you've failed time and time again, take some time to truly reflect on it. Who were you in those situations and those instances? Were you focused on bringing out the best in yourself and bringing joy and gratitude to the world? Or was your mindset continually reminding yourself that you weren't good enough? That you hadn't done enough?

Because the first step to the life you've always dreamed of is actually quite simple. Give yourself a break. The constant reminders in your head of what you aren't and what you don't have are not helpful. They actively detract from your ability to find success and happiness.

EMERGING FROM FAILURE

In hindsight, the truth was that framing all these life lessons as failures was part of the problem. To truly chart a new course in your life, you must let go of the narrative in your head that tells you you're not good enough and aren't doing enough.

You need to let that part of yourself go for a very simple reason. It doesn't help.

That's the key.

I remember running down the West Side Highway with my friend Scott talking about firings and failures. He commented, "I always thought you had an amazing career and was also so impressed by the different roles you'd taken."

I instantly countered, "No, they've all been failures. I haven't achieved the thing you're supposed to achieve working for all these startups, which is a liquidity event. I haven't made it."

He replied, "Does it help?"

"Does what help?"

"The constant disapproval of yourself. The constant negative energy you bring to every interaction. Does it make people want to be around you more? Does it help you at work to close deals or achieve your goals?"

And the answer, of course, was no. It doesn't help.

Even if you don't believe any of it. Even if you are convinced that deep down inside you really are worthless and a failure. The reality is that all of that doesn't help you get where you want to go. And telling yourself what you can't do or haven't done is a surefire way to ensure that you won't do it.

As Henry Ford said, "Whether you think you can or you can't, you're right."

I'd reached that point in my life, finally, where after so many repeated setbacks, both real and imagined, I was ready to try something new.

That something new was straightforward and is something anybody can do, including you. I was going to take a chance, and I was going to start believing in myself.

Sitting there in that moment, the thing that shifted wasn't a business plan or some amazing new app I could create. It was the resolution, formed from years of setbacks and negative energy, that this time would be different. I would not give my happiness or my pride to others anymore. I was going to take a leap, based on belief in myself, and I was going to break the pattern that had been consistent inside of me since childhood.

REFRAMING YOUR NARRATIVE

The reality, in hindsight, and writing this from years in the future when I've realized so many of my wildest and most extravagant dreams, is that the biggest failure of all was classifying my life as a failure in the first place. That was the critical flaw.

The path forward to not just success but to fulfillment begins when you reframe the story you tell yourself about your life.

The New Testament (I'm Jewish but there's wisdom all over the place, and I'll take it where I find it) says: "For to everyone who has will more be given, and he will have abundance; but from him who has not, even what he has will be taken away."

A story of your life that frames your experiences and your setbacks as stones on a journey leading to fulfillment will change the flow of energy around you and begin to attract more success. Success breeds success, and abundance breeds abundance.

In 2017, I resolved that being fired from The Muse was not going to be a setback. Instead, I simply resolved it would be a springboard. That I would emerge from this experience more powerful and more confident, and that I would leap into the void of entrepreneurship and trust that I would land on my feet. I would bet on myself.

I decided I would discard the narrative that I needed to "regroup" or I needed to "nurse my wounds." I wasn't going to take a vacation. I didn't need to stare at the ocean and feel bad or sorrow or self-pity. While I knew I was human, and had depressive tendencies anyway, this time I would harness the certainty and the strength I knew was within me and I would use it to forge a new path, one where I made more of the rules, and one where I confirmed to myself that I was who I had always hoped and thought I was.

There was nothing exterior that needed to happen. All of the things that would later completely change my life and produce so many incredible results. All of that simply started within myself. And it started simply by deciding it was so. Deciding it was so and letting go of the story I'd been telling myself that I was a failure in the first place and that I wasn't capable of what I knew I was capable of.

THE PATH FORWARD

So how do you change your life? How do you reset if you feel like you keep running into a wall? Well, there's no simple formula. But for me the first step was resetting the narrative inside my head. Failures are experiences, and I learned something from every one of them.

Part of the ability to view the world through that lens is to have an appropriate perspective on time. One of the famous maxims in technology is that people overestimate what can be done in a quarter and underestimate what can be done in a decade.

If you take a short-term transactional view of your life and your career, and feel a deep sense of pressure, anxiety, and urgency to do something amazing very quickly, then failure may well fill your field of vision.

I remember getting out of the University of Virginia and telling anyone who would listen that I needed to be worth $12.8 million by the time I was 28. I have no idea why I picked that number—it sounded big to me at the time. I was about 23 when I was saying that and the only thing that could possibly make me that wealthy was my record label if it somehow became something it was not. And it did not become that thing.

That sense of pressure—to be something amazing or to accomplish something amazing *in such a short period of time* was a contributing factor to my sense of defeat. It's a very good thing to want great things for yourself and to use tools and techniques, which we'll discuss to help you achieve them.

But the *need*—the need to have those things and to achieve that greatness in such a short period of time is a complicating factor.

I wrote in the introduction to "play a long big game." If you are able to take a longer-term view of your life and your contributions to the world, not only can you achieve something amazing and have greater happiness on a day-to-day basis but you can also create more space for serendipity and for wonder. A "small short game" is thinking about life transactionally. It's chiseling. It restricts you. It limits who you are and what you're capable of. Having a long-term view, removing the need from your daily life, removing the grind and the frustration and the resentment, if you can do that, you can set yourself free.

There's a good reason for the clichés "Life is a marathon, not a sprint" and "It's the journey, not the destination."

One of the keys to personal and professional success is very much to process and absorb the idea that the moment, right now, is beautiful and wonderful and no better or worse than any other moment. This moment as we know is all we have.

So letting go of need. Putting it down. Recasting a lack of having as failure and disregarding arbitrary short-term thinking for more relaxed and easy long-term thinking is part of the path to success.

As I thought about my next steps, my mind was no longer concerned with a "get rich quick" scheme. The energy around constantly trying to sprint to a milestone only to have that milestone disappear and evaporate with every firing had left me. I was spent. And as a result of being spent, I was able to let go. And not need anything from the moment save for what it gave me. If this sounds pretentious or mystical it's likely a bit of both. There's so much of Buddhism in true paths to happiness, and this is maybe some watered-down version of it.

The next step was to use that experience. But use that experience to listen to the market and find something that aligned with the path of the universe. Work with the wind not against it. The third step was to take a leap. A leap of faith and of trust that I was capable of becoming who I'd always hoped to be and wanted to be.

CHAPTER 1 TACTICS: NEGOTIATING SEVERANCE

Before we wrap up and talk about how you can reframe lessons of failure and chart a new and different course for yourself, I want to make sure that I leave you with some very practical tips and tricks for your career that you can leverage.

There's a lot that's going to be wishy-washy in this book and will require some deep mental and spiritual self-evaluation. But in every chapter I want to make sure I also leave you with something super-actionable and tactical.

One key element that has changed my life as a startup executive is having the foresight to pre-negotiate severance before you take your next job. For most high-growth companies, they'll pay you some severance when you're fired. But please understand that severance is *not required* to be paid. It is optional, and you'll have to sign a bunch of releases and other paperwork if you do get it. The market rate is typically three months of base pay for a vice president–level candidate or above.

However, at Pavilion, we coach our executives to first pre-negotiate severance as part of your employment negotiation. And we coach people to target a minimum of 6 months of severance with a goal of 12, paid in one lump sum (vs. paid with payroll).

Many companies will balk at the very idea of mentioning severance in the first place. They'll try to play psychology with you. "Why are we talking about severance when you haven't even started?" Perhaps in the same way that a potential marital partner might balk at a prenup and employ guilt in that discussion.

We have talk tracks we can give you, and the happy benefit of them is that they're all true. Namely that the average tenure for executives is short, that you're taking a huge chance with your life by taking on a new role, and that this is simply the reality of what you need to do in the modern workforce.

But however you get there, do try and get there. Prior to my success with Pavilion, my biggest financial liquidity events all came from pre-negotiated severance. It can give you breathing room to find your next job, and if it's pre-negotiated, you can go to work with a little lighter step every day knowing that you've anticipated some of the negative outcomes and have properly planned for them.

If the company truly won't grant you the 6 month's severance, you can counter with a time-based increase in severance starting at 3 months for perhaps the first 6–12 months and moving to 6 months or greater after having demonstrated tenure with the firm.

The more you can pre-negotiate, the less anxiety you'll feel if you sense the winds are changing at work and start to feel unsteady. I learned this after getting fired from Axial and, in my last full-time job before working on what would become Pavilion, I negotiated 12 months of severance on a $400,000 base salary. That $400,000 was effectively the seed capital for the business and gave me enough runway to get the business to a point where it could pay my salary within a few months.

So, yes, we'll talk about all manner of recovering from failure but if you're on an executive track, one thing to always target is pre-negotiating six months of severance for any VP-level job or greater.

CHAPTER 2

The Exit Ramp

I'll be back in a few hours.

I said this to Camille, my wife, on my way out the door to meet my CEO. It was the Monday after I'd had my epiphany on the New Jersey Turnpike, or at the very least a steeling of my resolve. On a walk around the block with my CEO, I was told to leave. Just as I expected. And I was back home in a few hours with my wife as promised.

In some ways, that was the best walk around the block I'd ever taken. It was the springboard for everything that's happened since. I was ready to reframe the narrative of my life and take control of where I was headed. I wouldn't let this break me. I would come out stronger. I knew it.

TURNING FAILURE INTO OPPORTUNITY

Self-perception and narratives have such a hold over us. We all see ourselves as the star in our story, after all. But, we're also quick to see the worst in ourselves. To let doubt creep in and fear take over.

As I realized at the rest stop, the story of your life, the narrative that you tell yourself, can be determinative. Part of what finally clicked for me was that I didn't need to be the victim anymore. That I was stronger than I'd given myself credit for and that it was time to take a bet on myself and truly leap into the void of starting my own business and making my own money.

Before this revelation, I thought everyone would look down on me for being fired. Again. Or that anyone who told me it would be fine was lying. But once I viewed myself in a positive light, I could see that my reputation was better than I thought. My network was more open and willing to help than I had previously believed. I had more opportunities than I ever thought possible.

I remember the realization I had in the days and weeks after that penultimate firing, thinking to myself, "Somehow I've emerged from this experience more powerful than when I went into it."

Failure is a framing. Success is a framing. As my father would routinely tell me, there were people who emerged from the Holocaust and, because they survived, considered themselves the luckiest people on the planet, even perhaps after losing their entire families and suffering unspeakable tragedy. And there are people who are late for an appointment or misplace their car keys and think they've suffered unspeakable loss and can't bear to face the day.

And, again referencing and paraphrasing Henry Ford, both of those people are correct. Your life is whatever story you tell yourself. And the most important point is that what you tell yourself—that story—is YOUR CHOICE.

It may not feel like it at times, but it is. If you consider yourself a loser, you are. If you consider yourself a winner, you are. We speak our reality into existence.

So I went home after my walk-about with my now former CEO and told myself a new story. One where I got to work and started building something for myself that didn't depend on the whims of others. A fresh page where I could map out the life I've always wanted. And it all started with recognizing the power of experience.

THE POWER OF EXPERIENCE

The point of sharing my story isn't to say you should start your own company. This book is about finding the greatness within yourself and finding a way to bring it out into the world and giving you a framework for doing that. For realizing your dreams and becoming the person you believe you are inside.

For me, that journey led to Pavilion and achieving all the things I'd dreamt about for so many years. For you it may be something else. The point is that you are the author of your own narrative.

Experience is learned the hard way. From doing things right and succeeding—and doing things wrong and failing. Starting a business was the outcome of the years of experience I had leading up to that point. The time and purpose was right for me in 2017.

At that point, I'd been working for 18 years. I'd worked at high-growth companies that had succeeded, and I'd played a part. I'd also worked in companies that wanted to succeed, but didn't have the right formula. I'd had term sheets pulled. I'd been fired. I'd made the right hires. And some wrong ones, too—like the time I brought in a new sales manager to run the team who spent an hour talking about himself and why he loved Billy Joel concerts. He immediately lost the trust and credibility of the team and damaged my credibility in the process. (I also got the strong feeling that despite being a family man he had a bad drug problem. But I digress.)

As discussed in Chapter 1, all those so-called failures were really building blocks for later success. But only if I took a long enough view on my life and my career to see them as such.

If I needed success right away, if every experience had to be the one that put me on top of the mountain, then failures were just failures. But if I could be patient and not need anything in the moment, but simply trust that the path I was taking would lead me somewhere good if I approached it from a place of genuine curiosity, empathy, and compassion, then those life lessons could be experiences. And experiences could lead me to success.

Fresh out of school, many people prioritize money and glory. They want to climb the ladder quickly to a bigger salary and a more impressive title. I know I did.

But a career is a long-term play. You'll never reach your full potential if you don't have a wealth of experiences to guide you. The first stage of your career is the time to gain as much experience as possible. Choosing bad companies early can actually give you powerful insights to avoid costly mistakes in the latter stages of your career. So don't be afraid to take a job for the experience. To try something new. And absorb as much knowledge as you can.

I came home from my final firing ready to get to work, but I needed to figure out what work I wanted to do and how to get started. It all started with getting my expertise on paper.

THE POWER OF DOCUMENTING YOUR EXPERTISE

One of the best pieces of advice I received was from Camille. I got home from my last day at The Muse and told her I wanted to start a consulting company, but didn't know precisely where to start. She said, "Write down everything you know about building and running a company. Why don't you start there?"

A brilliant piece of advice.

I opened my laptop and let the knowledge flow. I typed all of the elements that I knew made for a successful company. Different decisions on pricing, on team design, on compensation, on functional roles within an organization.

All at once, all of my failures transformed into critical tools, ultimately becoming a diagnostic tool I leveraged in my consulting work. That diagnostic tool then turned into a consulting product I could sell to CEOs and companies, and this led me to meeting founders, investors, and others who needed help.

More and more, it dawned on me that helping others was what I was meant to do. I was actively rewriting my narrative as I jotted down lessons from all these experiences I'd had—experiences I'd previously deemed failures. I could harness all I'd gone through and help others succeed.

If you're not sure where you want to go, the process of documentation is a useful and important step to help you understand your status quo. What are the things you've learned over the years, and how can you classify and structure them into a usable system to guide you forward?

My diagnostic tool ended up being an almost 600-question survey I would use to evaluate companies against 144 different sub-categories of excellence, rolling up into 21 super-categories, and culminating in one specific grade every company could receive and benchmark themselves against to understand their performance. The result had objective criteria and became an interesting and useful piece of intellectual property as I looked to build out my consulting business and ended up generating a pipeline of well over six figures in just a matter of weeks.

Of course, the diagnostic tool was useless if nobody knew it existed, which was why the second step of my journey wasn't just writing down everything I knew but calling everyone I knew.

THE POWER OF MAINTAINING YOUR NETWORK

I picked up the phone and started dialing. I called old colleagues. Executive search firms I'd worked with at places like True and Daversa and Kindred. Old investors I'd known from places like Comcast Ventures or Edison Ventures. Old CEOs. Anyone who might be interested in hearing how I was doing. Anyone who might be able to help. Anyone who I might be able to help. I would give them an update, I would tell them about what I was doing, and I would see where the breadcrumb trail would lead.

I hoped every call would turn into at least one additional call with someone else, or somewhere and at some point I would find an opportunity to market my new diagnostic tool and make some money of my own.

It sounds simple, and yet so many people don't take this obvious step. As some people say, your network is your net worth.

But this never would have worked if I hadn't actively maintained my network over the years. Maintaining your network isn't just calling people when you need something. It's about offering to help them without asking anything in return. It's about finding specific, thoughtful ways you can support them. It's about rooting for them and lifting them up through their downs, then celebrating their wins.

Pavilion is built on this same mentality of reciprocity, or give to get. You should always look to give, whether it's your time, expertise, or connecting a friend with someone else in your network. Only by giving will we get anything in return from our network.

In fact, that's really the only mechanism through which I view networking. As I've shared with our Members many times, I loathe happy hours. I don't want to just bump into random people and make small talk. I'm an introvert, and happy hours suck the energy from me.

No, when I do networking, I am simply looking to help someone. That's it. I am looking to do anything I can to help them, and, importantly, I'm not keeping score. I'm not tabulating the value of my help and sending them an invoice. I am helping them with no expectation of anything in return.

I can't stress this enough, and you'll read about this in a variety of different ways throughout the book. But if you're reading these words now, please, please stop keeping score. Look to help. That's the trick. That's the secret.

The point of this book is that giving is not a detour on the path to success. It IS the path to success. Burn that into your brain and you'll have embraced one of the core concepts that's led me here.

For me, maintaining my network meant being good to other folks and seeing where I could help them. I liked helping people, and it gave me a good feeling about myself.

So when I started calling folks, I realized they liked me, too. That they remembered when I'd been useful or helpful, and many were eager to do the same in return. Importantly, I didn't go into a call with expectations. I didn't need anything from that call. The goal was simply to explain my situation, let them know that I was building my consulting business, and see if they knew anybody that might benefit from a conversation.

And something amazing happened as I worked through my call list and paced my living room, wearing grooves into my floor. Somehow, some way, I'd emerged from this "failure" more powerful and in a better place than ever before.

Undoubtedly the years of hard work I'd put into helping other people had made a difference, because so many people were eager and happy to take my call, eager to help make introductions, eager to vouch for me, eager to help.

My very first consulting project came from a call with my good friend Rishi and a breakfast with another friend, Jordan. Both, separately, mentioned this interesting company called LeagueApps that provided software for youth sports organizations. They had just fired their VP of sales, and needed assistance on their go-to-market. That led to introductions to the co-founders, Brian Litvack, the CEO, and Jeremy Goldberg, the president.

Both ended up being great people and were nodding along as I laid out my idea for a five-day diagnostic process in which I would interview their sales and marketing teams, identify gaps and areas of opportunity using my framework, and help them assess what they needed to move forward.

I quoted $12,000 and they countered with $10,000. I accepted, and just like that I had my first client. We signed the agreement on November 6—a little over two weeks after I was fired.

That's how quickly success can happen if you bring the right mindset. The right mindset is not simply one of determination, although that is part of it. It was also about reframing my narrative, refusing to be the victim, not giving in to feelings of self-pity or self-loathing, and then doing the work.

And part of the work was about approaching interactions with other people without a direct need and without desperation. It wasn't about one specific person to talk to or one specific outcome. It was about the process of managing and maintaining a network and looking for opportunities to have non-transactional, long-term relationships and connections with others.

PLAYING FOR THE LONG TERM

A theme of my life and of my perspective on what can drive a different kind of professional success revolves around the notion of long-term thinking.

As I mentioned above, early in your career is the time for experiences. But long-term thinking goes beyond that. If you look at your career in the long term, you'll see that mid-career is when you should start leveraging all of your experiences to take on more responsibility. That responsibility leads to the title. And that leads to wealth. Focusing on the long term and building up your career is a distinct competitive advantage in a world that is so short-term oriented.

There's an element of spirituality and faith in long-term thinking because it relies on a fundamentally positive view of existence and the universe, at least within the framework of regulated capitalism—and for things that are not tragedies completely outside of your control.

But within the lens of things that are generally within your control, you can benefit from taking a much longer-term view of the world and of your career.

Part of the reason that long-term thinking benefits you is because it relieves you of desperation and need. If you can enter interactions and transactions without the need to be paid back or be rewarded, without the cloying desperation that need imposes upon you, then you can find serendipity and positivity in chance encounters.

And if you can think for the long term, you can do things for people without needing an immediate return. There are so many reasons why this can benefit you from a selfish perspective, and, as one of those again that I think about, a big one is that so few people do it.

So many people have been taught to "never split the difference" and "don't leave money on the table." So much of business philosophy is about maximizing value extraction and not about thinking about value creation from a long-term, relationship-based perspective.

In each interaction it might be okay to leave money on the table or to do things for people that don't require immediate payback. The fundamentally selfish reason it's okay is because the long-term value creation you get from a warm and supportive relationship can be many factors bigger than the short-term gain you might get from ensuring you chisel people for every nickel they might have.

Like when I got my first consulting job through my network. That wasn't because I cold-called someone once. That was the result of years of relationship-building and support without expectations. And when the time came that I was the one who needed support, my network was there for me.

Life is not a zero-sum game. There's room for all of us to win, and leaning toward kindness and giving and sharing can actually help you reap even bigger rewards than being cutthroat.

THE EXIT RAMP

It's important to note that the exit ramp for me or for you might be different. The exit we are taking is off the meta-phorical shit-stain that is the New Jersey Turnpike of transactionalism, fear, anxiety, and failure so that we can take a different road that delivers personal satisfaction and contentment over the course of your life.

It doesn't necessarily mean that you should immediately start your own company or quit your job. But what it does mean is that you can take an intentional actualized view of your life and yourself and choose to live not in fear, desperation, or need, but act from a place of contentment and abundance.

For me, that contentment needed to come from my own independence from these forces. I needed to break free from the traditional dictates of work and transactionalism, and I needed to gain confidence in my own abilities to forge a path for myself, independent of others.

As I said, this decision was intentional and, as a consequence, empowered. By hook or by crook, I was going to make my own money, even if that meant reducing the urgency to make a specific amount of money or to achieve some specific world-changing goal by a certain date. That pressure often comes from the influence of investors and venture capital into businesses, and it forecloses the opportunity to take things organically. They assume that capital is the key constraint and that a harried, frenzied, anxious approach to growth is the best possible route to success.

I'm here to tell you that it's not.

REFLECT ON YOUR JOY

A long-term view is useful because it underscores the value of experience and resets failure into learning. Learning and experience translate into judgment, and over time, you use that judgment to make better decisions.

But to take an exit ramp, you have to be on the highway.

The point that I'm making is that I want you to achieve joy and happiness and contentment in your life, and I think there is a path to doing that from the moment you join the workforce. In that sense, the exit ramp is simply a metaphor for employing a different perspective on how you want to behave, what you need from other people, and what values you want to embody.

But in another sense, the sequencing is important, and you can't leverage experience if you don't have any. Which means that you may need to delay ultimate professional satisfaction so that you can develop and gain the experiences you'll need to achieve that satisfaction and success in the first place.

So many people advise you to "do what you love," but as I learned at my failed record label, that does not mean you will have a successful career. And that way of thinking can be problematic. Maybe you've never experienced any happiness at all in life and that spills over to your work. Or you may have misdefined certain activities such that you missed how they might contribute.

But on your journey it is important to be on the lookout. Saying "do what you love" is silly if you don't know what you love. And again you may fall victim to misdefinition. Still, you should watch for the things that give you joy. To understand those moments when you feel flow, or when you feel transported, or when you feel that sense of fulfillment and maybe nobody is even paying you for it.

My favorite easy way to articulate this is to be in tune with your body and understand what activities or people bring you energy and which sap your energy. If you can be in tune with and aware of the things you're doing that bring you energy, you can optimize for those activities over time.

Over the years while I'd been toiling away as a "Chief Revenue Officer" at all these various startups, I had found flow, but I'd found it in strange places. My greatest sense of satisfaction came from helping people I cared about. Helping means a lot of things when it comes to the workplace. It could be a piece of advice, or it could be a valuable introduction.

Beginning in 2014, I started hosting regular dinners and meetups. It began with an admonition from one of my colleagues, Joanna Curran. She'd said, "Put yourself at the center of something." And that inspired me. It inspired me to start hosting meetups and talks, and bringing people together to share common ground. Those meetups translated into quarterly dinners where we'd all show up at Rosa Mexicana or a sushi place near Union Square to talk shop.

It's funny because I consider myself an introvert. Or perhaps an ambivert. Regardless, I don't get energy from generalized human interactions. But somehow I do get energy from time-bound, focused human interactions with a purpose.

But ambivert, extrovert, introvert, or whatever other vert, I'd been hosting dinners for over three years when I was fired from The Muse and when I was pacing around my apartment on speakerphone.

I'd always believed that random meetings don't really do very much if the people who attend those meetings can't convene in between the meetings to share thoughts and maintain the momentum of their conversations.

To that end, we'd all been on a group email thread since 2014 where everyone was in the To: line. But after a while, that seemed onerous, and furthermore it could cost confidentiality and intimacy if people's thoughts were directly forwarded from their email addresses.

In 2016, I gave that email thread a name and created a Google Group to house and archive the conversations. That name was "The New York Revenue Collective." That name eventually became Pavilion and changed my life, but more importantly, it eventually helped tens of thousands of people change the trajectory of their lives and careers for the better.

And yet, in the moment, I was just having fun and doing what I liked to do. It's only in hindsight that all of this falls into place as a logical narrative. It didn't at the time.

At the time it was simply joyful.

Some part of me derives so much genuine satisfaction from making an introduction between two people and hearing back weeks later, "I got a job!" or "I hired them!" or some other meaningful productive outcome. I didn't need to be paid to do that—I didn't even consider that it might be possible to get paid to do that—it just felt so good.

Helping others experience happiness and joy—that's what powers me. Even before I had a name for it or a philosophy or anything like that.

When people approach me, asking, "How did you do it?" it's hard to answer. I originally approached this work with no need and no expectations. Sure, I'd always thought I'd be a better CEO than the people I was reporting to, but all I ever really wanted was freedom and independence. I didn't *need* to be the CEO if we were winning and achieving great things.

But the foundation of the company that I've built since then was not born from an MBA lecture or an incubator or some structured attempt at world domination. It was built from sincere joy. The joy that I derived from creating things, creating experiences for people, watching them enjoy those experiences, and finding success based on the infrastructure I'd provided and the guidance and help I'd lent.

It took a long time, and it happened from love and not from need. It happened because I took an exit ramp, but only after I'd had the years of experience and wisdom that I needed to make that decision intentionally and with purpose.

If you're not ready to strike out on your own, that's okay. Life is not about immediately taking huge risks and throwing caution to the wind, particularly when you might be in a situation with fewer options.

But along your journey, you should trust that goodness will find you if you're open to it. Look for the small activities, moments, and interactions that ultimately fill you up. Start to catalog and classify them as you go. Build up an archive. Because those moments of joy are clues about the true path of happiness for yourself and for others.

And for me I discovered my joy when I was building something that made no money and had no ulterior motive, save for bringing people together and helping them achieve their own goals. I did this explicitly with the hope that some great thing would happen to them and they didn't need to do anything for me in return.

The joy I found in giving led to the set of values foundational to Pavilion, and those values have powered us for many years as we've grown.

YOU ARE NOT A VICTIM

At the core of all of these decisions lies an underlying assumption. That I actually *did* have control over my life. That's important to underscore and stress.

Part of your path to happiness—part of the ability to experience happiness in the first place—is a belief that you have control.

And it's true that logically free will is an impossibility. But even if we all die and go wherever we're going and they tell us that free will was always a myth, life is better and more fulfilling if we believe it exists.

If you believe that you control what happens, how you feel, and what you think, you have a sense of independence and autonomy that itself can bring you joy. It's why those small acts of creation like creating a Google Group for the New York Revenue Collective were so fulfilling to me, because it confirmed my suspicion that I was in control of my life.

So as we play for the long term and look to bring happiness into our lives, we must correspondingly assume that we have that power in the first place.

It sounds simple, but for so many people it's not. Do you know folks who are constantly complaining about things happening to them? As if they play no role? My family always jokes that in Spanish the construction of the sentence defrays responsibility and blame. "*Se me cayo*" literally means "it fell to me" as opposed to "I dropped it."

We have to dispense with that construction if we are to have a meaningful life. The universe is a pattern of energy upon which you can imprint your desires and your wishes, but to do that you have to believe that you actually have that control in the first place.

So one of the first steps in taking the exit ramp is to dispense with victimhood. You are not a victim. Most of the things that happened in your life were a result of decisions you made and the manner in which you behaved.

There were and are things that I've done over the years that caused me to be fired. The way I behaved and the mind-set I brought to my job. Those were my choices. I was not "unlucky." In fact, the reality is that I consider myself incredibly lucky. And I am so grateful for every failure I've ever had and every negative experience because they brought me to where I am now.

So let's ensure that you're not telling yourself a sad story with you as the victim. You weren't unlucky. You make your own luck. And even if it's not true, it's a better way to live when you believe that you do.

The conceit of living this way is that you have power over your future and the outcomes you generate. And just as importantly, whatever results you've generated in the past have been a result of your actions and behaviors and not simply someone else's fault or problem. Again, you are not the victim.

I appreciate that there are so many factors contributing to whether this is in fact true. And there are societal constructs and biases that have definitely impacted your ability to get where you want to go. I am not denying those realities. This is saying that blaming your results on outside forces isn't *useful* to you. That's the point. Being a victim doesn't help you get where you want to go.

Part of taking the exit ramp is dispensing with the idea that you are a victim of circumstances. That you are any kind of victim at all. Take ownership of who you are and where you want to go, and you'll get there.

RELEASE THE PRESSURE

I was recently on the phone with a Pavilion Member who was anxious that life was passing him by. Anxious that he'd been in the startup land, grinding it out for years as a chief revenue officer and didn't have enough to show for it. His company had just been sold, and he'd worked there for years. The founder and CEO made gobs of money, but my Member had only made a little, and he was frustrated. He was feeling like it was finally time to set out on his own and be the founder himself.

He'd been incubating a product in the insurance industry with a technical co-founder and had been iterating and testing it for months. Unfortunately, nothing was working.

He felt strongly that he wanted to be a CEO and founder; he just didn't know of what.

The problem with this approach to entrepreneurship is that it's based on you and not the universe. It's not built around joy. It's built around anxiety and resentment and an inordinate pressure that now is the time that something must be done to make your life meaningful and purposeful.

And that's not, in my experience, where true greatness comes from.

I told my friend to stick it out. To stop focusing on "being a founder" and start having more conversations with potential customers. Pick a category that you're passionate about. Pick a problem that you're consumed with solving. Pick something you've found joy working on. Those are the criteria for finding something meaningful and purposeful.

That joy that we seek in controlling our destiny eludes us when we apply too much pressure to ourselves around what we're supposed to be and by when, and the anxiety comes from insecurity around our place in the world.

The leap of faith into the unknown must be powered by joy, not desperation. It needs to be a positive, unbending belief that propels you forward, not a cloying desperation that you're not where you're supposed to be.

So how do you do that?

Well, it starts by releasing the pressure yourself. Remember that I used to state publicly that by 28 I was going to be worth $12.8 million. I have no idea where that came from. It was 1999 during the dot-com boom, and I was determined to prove to people that if I just said something loudly that would make it true.

It was a dumb thing to say and a weird goal to have because it didn't have anything to do with anything. It didn't come from experience. It didn't come from wisdom. It didn't come from any specific point of view on how to help people or what I could do for them. It was just a statement about my own insecurity and my personal fear that I was insignificant in the eyes of the universe.

Twenty-eight came and went, and I wasn't worth anything close to $12.8 million. What I did do at 28 was begin a marriage that ended in bitterness, poverty, and heartbreak. I certainly didn't have a ton of money to show for it.

Saying "I need to be a CEO" or "I need to start something" comes from a similar place. A place that's only about you.

Those kinds of impractical outcome-focused goals, without a plan, and without any kind of external focus on helping other people, are bound to fail. And they derive from the intense pressure we all feel to be significant within a certain time frame.

I'm not saying you're not going to be significant. You will be—if you come from the right place, and reset your destination around what truly gives you purpose, and if you release the pressure from every decision.

Trust your gut, trust your intuition, and believe that if you live relatively well you'll be alive a long time. You can start a business in your fifties. You can change the world in your sixties. Robert Altman didn't direct his first movie until his forties.

In *Super Founders: What Data Reveals About Billion-Dollar Startups* (2021), Ali Tamaseb revealed that the founders of eventual unicorns had a median age of 34 when they started their businesses. More broadly, *Harvard Business Review* reported in 2018 that 45 was the average age at which a successful founder started their company.

There is time. There is plenty of time.

And, again, even if there isn't, it is far more useful to believe there is. This isn't about a lack of urgency. This is about not needing just to need. The more you need, the more desperately you want, and the less you'll get.

That's how the universe works, unfortunately.

Don't contort yourself into a pretzel based on bland generalities and aphorisms. You don't need to do anything by any certain time, save for the time that your heart stops beating. You can have children in your forties or fifties. Look at that woman from the *Real Housewives of Atlanta*. Science can do wonderful things. You can strike it rich late in life. There is no timetable.

I'm not saying be average or that you should have to accept that you might be mediocre. That's not true. I believe in your greatness, whoever you are.

I remember my therapist once tried to talk me out of these feelings by telling me that feeling special or different didn't mean I had something great inside me, it meant I had a personality flaw from childhood.

I'm not saying that at all.

You DO have greatness within you. I'm saying the way to bring that greatness out from inside yourself is not by exerting undue pressure, but by releasing the pressure and trusting that if you discover joy and grace and compassion and love, good things truly will happen even if you don't quite know exactly how or why.

Some of my happiest times in life were sitting at my little white desk from West Elm in the corner of a rundown apartment on 8th Avenue and 12th Street in 2020, the middle of the pandemic, sending emails to our Members. Revenue Collective, the company that became Pavilion, grew five times during the pandemic. It was miraculous.

And yet on any given day I wasn't focused on any specific kind of growth metric. I was focused on finding joy. I removed the pressure from myself that I had to earn anything more than what I needed to pay my bills and pay my rent. And from there I could move up Maslow's pyramid to self-actualization.

So if you're thinking about taking a leap, striking out on your own, think first about what your motivation is. Think about whether you can afford to go for a long stretch without money. Think about if you're coming from insecurity or desperation, or if you're coming from contentment and joy.

I told my friend who wanted to be a founder to stay at his job. Thinking you should be a founder or CEO isn't enough. It's not coming from the right place, especially if you don't have any kind of insights about the market. Don't frame it as "I need to start something." Frame it as "I found a problem that a lot of people have and I love solving for them."

Don't mistake it for complacency. The exit ramp is not about accepting mediocrity. We will still do our thing. We will still work hard and bring urgency and intensity and resolve to our daily lives—but we'll do it from a different place. Not a place of need or competition, but a place of peace.

Once we've made the decision to start playing by a different set of rules, ones based on kindness, compassion, and helping others, we can begin to reset our destination.

CHAPTER 2 TACTICS: LESSONS OF CONSULTING

There is no job security in the modern world. There is no security really of any kind. The world is an uncertain place. We know that, of course. So part of the theme of this book, of my philosophy, is that you need to build up sources of income for yourself that are independent of employers. Advising and consulting are great things once you have the experience.

And one of the reasons consulting and advising are great is because you can use those opportunities to talk to a wide variety of customers and people to understand their problems. Solving those problems for them might lead to an idea or a framework or a solution that could turn into a company or a product.

When you're consulting, there's only one way to scale (unless you want to hire a bunch of people, which can be a pain in the ass). That way is to charge more money for less time, since time is your only asset.

The advice I give is to avoid charging by the hour if possible and instead charge for "products." One of the first things I did for my consulting business was build out a diagnostic tool that would assess how well a company was positioned to grow. This was the "product" I sold to LeagueApps and it was priced at $12,000 for four days (although we settled on $10,000). $12,000 for four days is a $3,000 day rate. That's a lot of money for a lot of people, but I never quoted my services by the hour or by the day. I quoted them by my product.

Eventually I raised the price to $15,000, and I cut the time to three days, and all of a sudden I had a $5,000 day rate, growing my implied revenue per project by 65% on a per day basis. Presto changeo.

If you need access to some of the materials I used, we provide them free to all our Pavilion Members. Just ask. Feel free to copy, modify, or steal in any way you want if it's helpful.

CHAPTER 3

Reset Your Destination

What do you stand for?

The months leading up to that fateful day at that rest stop on the New Jersey Turnpike were filled with anxiety. An uneasy feeling in the pit of my stomach I couldn't shake. Even before my rest stop epiphany, I had an innate sense that something needed to change. I couldn't keep going like this.

So I'd sought out a coach to help me take some different steps in life. Emmanuelle Skala, one of the great revenue leaders in startup land, had suggested I reach out to her coach, Jim Rosen.

We got on our first video conference, and Jim came on the screen and we got to chatting. He innocently asked me, "What do you stand for?"

My mind went blank.

"Making money?" I said.

"That's not enough," he said. "What do you stand for besides making money?"

I didn't have an answer. And that's when the panic started to set in. If I didn't know what I stood for, how could I build something great? What will it be about? Who will it be for? What was I even doing with my life?

It's not enough to stand for "making money." In fact, it doesn't really answer the question in the first place. Making money is the output of building something wonderful. It's not prescriptive. It's ultimately empty and means nothing.

You make money when you build something that reflects who you are, what you stand for, and your values. All of that needs to come from a place of joy and fulfillment.

Money is the natural outcome of that process in regulated capitalism (the most beautiful system in the history of mankind, in my opinion).

So standing for making money wasn't enough. Jim pointed that out for me. But in BRS (before the rest stop) time, it was a puzzling moment for me. What did I stand for?

THE ELUSIVE STRUGGLE FOR MONEY

I'd suffered through so much cynicism and defeat in the previous 10 years. The culture of my first company, Gerson Lehrman Group (GLG), had been so much about making money in those old days. And the clients we'd served, hedge funds, all had 20- and 30-something millionaires getting huge bonuses for their trades and their investment positions. Twenty-eight-year-olds driving Ferraris around the Hamptons and Connecticut. God, I was jealous.

I'd had a few years back at GLG where they'd written me some very large checks. Like back in 2006 and 2007, I made close to $800,000 after Silver Lake Partners invested over $200 million with us, and I was paid a retention bonus as a key person on the account.

Coming out of GLG, in the midst of a financially costly and emotionally tragic divorce, all that money I'd made had been bled out of me slowly by lawyers and my ex-wife. All things in life are correlated, and so often there are macro forces beyond our control or reach. While I know now that looking at yourself as a victim does nothing to help, it's impossible to deny that sometimes we are part of something bigger. And at the time, victim was all I could see in myself.

So there I was during the 2008 and 2009 financial crisis with seemingly endless divorce costs, now making $700,000 less at my new company, Axial, and trying to reorient my entire life.

The "lesson" I'd taken from those days was simple: find a way to make money. Money is what matters. Work is a means to an end. And that end is to win the competition against your peers and friends. Win that competition of wealth and expensive watches and nice cars because those are the things that are important in life and especially when someone is trying to take it all from you.

I was completely blinded by this need to make more. To be more.

I'd spent a few months after I was fired from GLG trying to find what appeared to be a linear route from my perspective. Logically, I thought I should go work at a hedge fund where I could do for them internally what GLG did for them externally. I had a few meetings, but the reality was that I had no credible experience as any kind of head of research, and they would've had to teach me far too much to be useful. I wasn't a salesperson per se. I wasn't an investor. I was a service provider. And service providers generally don't get to be the ones who make it big.

So instead, I joined a startup. I learned a lot during my years building Axial, but money was always front and center for me. It was always dominant. I wanted nice things. My girlfriend, who later became my second wife, Camille, wanted nice things. It was a struggle. A grind.

Man, did we grind.

For years, all I could think about was money. I'm sure there are folks out there who understand. I was locked in this struggle. Eking things out. Spending more than I made. Negotiating for late payments on my maintenance to my ex-wife. Watching the credit card debt bounce around. Looking for shortcuts.

At one point, I'd become so desperate, I fell in with a con man from Germany full of talk and promises. He had contacts. He could sell cheap luxury items directly from retailers in Italy to some of the best e-commerce platforms in the United States, like Bluefly. Could I find someone to buy luxury handbags from his supplier? I could make 20%, he assured me.

I started networking with other e-commerce sites like Rue La La. I made the introductions, but as soon as I did, the guy would swoop in, steal the connection, and cut me out. We had a falling out when I accused him of being a fraud, but that was only after he made a couple hundred thousand dollars in sales from my contacts.

But still I couldn't stop. More credit card debt. Getting some kind of payment, but not paying taxes on it. Thinking if I could just make more money, tomorrow would never come.

But it would. I'd always have to pay the bill. Tax day would roll around, and my accountant would tell me I owed the IRS $60,000, and I would break down, knowing I didn't have it. Not at all.

Money clouded my brain for years.

On a trip to Italy years ago, all I could see were dollar signs. Every minute was like we were in an overpriced cab from the airport, watching the meter click. Dinner and drinks: $300. A boat to Capri: $250. Here's a nice little shopping detour in Paris: $500.

Coming home, I was terrified to log into American Express to see the butcher's bill. The bloody butcher's bill.

So, you see, when Jim Rosen asked me in 2017 what I stood for, I thought, "What kind of question is that?" I stood for paying off all the people who wanted something from me. I stood for making money. I stood for anxiety and stress and fear and bills I had to delay.

What else was there to stand for?

WHAT DO I STAND FOR?

And yet, that's why Jim and I did the exercise.

I hired Jim to help me navigate the treacherous waters that were The Muse and the sense of unease I had. I still ended up getting fired at the rest stop anyway, but Jim and I had already embarked on our journey together. I'd even negotiated Jim's fees as part of my severance package with The Muse.

If I cleared away the doubt and stress and anxiety, I sensed there was something deeper within me than just a desire to make money. We started looking at various attributes and qualities of a human being. I would circle those that resonated with me.

We ranked values against three key elements: foundation, focus, and future.

We started with the Foundation—what were my foundational values? What was important to me? We looked at values such as Honor, Respect, Discipline, and more to establish the foundation that was core to my survival.

From there, we looked at values that helped me Focus on who I was and helped me define my identity in a professional context more clearly.

Finally, we used those values to establish a vision for the Future—a vision for who I wanted to be.

The values most important to me were:

Support

Helpfulness

Loyalty

Appreciation

Altruism

Humor

Forgiveness

Mentoring

And all of it still centered around a concept of me as an architect of my future. One that valued achievement and impact over the course of a life.

The exercise was time consuming, but it was productive and useful. And at the end, I emerged with the realization that I did indeed stand for more than just making money. Much more.

From this values exercise, we wove together one coherent statement. My own personal mission statement. Something that I ultimately "stood for."

Simple, right? And maybe obvious, but at the time, it was a bit of an epiphany. One more milestone on my lifelong journey to transcendence.

> **I stand for helping people I care about and respect to achieve their goals.**

That mission statement is at the heart of the business I built. In fact, that IS the business I built. That's the whole point of Pavilion.

This statement helped me understand a core fact about myself: I draw strength and energy from helping people. Not just any people, but people I care about. Although, admittedly, I had a general tendency to care about most people I interacted with. But more than that, I feel fulfilled by helping people I respect.

And who I respect above all else are people who combine compassion with a work ethic. The kind of people who have the knowledge and wisdom to put their back into it and work hard, while still bringing compassion to their daily lives. The people who see the world as it is, understanding its trials and tribulations and tragedies, and still retain hope and optimism. People who I liked to think were like me.

Those are special people, and I want to do whatever I can to help those people achieve whatever it is they want to achieve.

And the funny thing was, when I looked behind me, reflecting on everything I'd done the past few years, that's exactly what I was already doing. I was already helping those people.

That's what the New York Revenue Collective was, after all. It was a series of dinners and emails all built around a simple concept—let's help each other. Maybe that could be the thing I stood for. Maybe that could be what drives me.

How to Reset Your Destination

Even just the fact of knowing and identifying what I stood for was a seminal moment for me, and it can be for you, too.

You have to know what you stand for. You don't have to stand for the same things I stand for. But you have to stand for something—something more than making money.

Money is the thing that follows *when* you pursue what you stand for. Your values are what will trigger the avalanche of money and success if you can find them and slowly, tirelessly work to align your reality with the vision of the world you want to see.

The problem for me in 2017, and the problem when I tried to give this advice to other people, was what you stand for doesn't always immediately translate into professional success. I had no way of knowing what would happen in the future. I didn't think it was possible that a small little networking business might be worth $200 million, or even $1 billion one day.

Unfortunately, that's how most things related to mental discipline and our relationship with the world function. We want everything to be as easy as pressing a button. Just hit it, and—poof! Your life changes instantly.

But that's the thing about playing for the long term and placing faith in something bigger than yourself: you need to trust that your values and ethics will someday lead to something great. It's a leap of faith, of sorts.

Leaps of faith are leaps because they aren't guaranteed. You need to trust that doing the right thing with the right structure will reward you, over time, in the ways that you've hoped. You need to believe it will happen.

But calling it a leap of faith for me isn't exactly fair or accurate. These were decisions made out of necessity and a sort of desperation.

I remember sitting at breakfast with my friend Jonathan Glick about a year later when I decided to pursue Revenue Collective (now Pavilion) full time. I said, "Well, if this doesn't work out, I can always go find another CRO job somewhere." He smiled at me indulgently, supportively, and said, "We've tried that experiment haven't we?"

I can't sit here and say, "It's a simple formula, my friend! Quit your job. Hire Jim Rosen. Do a values exercise. Soon, you'll be worth millions."

It's not about instant gratification. In fact, in many ways, it's about the exact opposite of instant gratification. It's about doing something for its own sake and not quitting your job or telling the man to fuck off just because (although that can feel very good).

It's about living a life according to your true principles. The main thing about charting a new destination is that it's a destination built on a different view of the world.

Don't get it twisted. Money still matters in this world. But it's a world inhabited by people willing to help you. Willing to support you. People who are willing to give you their time and not send you a bill the minute you hang up the phone. Doesn't that sound like the world you want to live in? Sometimes what we need is simply affirmation and confirmation that such a world can exist and that it's possible for us all to move toward a different universe.

When I was doing this exercise from my living room in the West Village on a Zoom with Jim Rosen, drawing squiggly lines between words like "Humor" and "Discipline" and "Compassion," I had no idea this would translate into anything directly. It wasn't about money, and it wasn't about instant reward of any kind or shape.

It was born from the intuition that there was a different way to conduct myself and that in order to get off the hamster wheel, I needed a series of frameworks and ideas that could help shift the trajectory of my life toward something more meaningful. Following the playbook others had set for me wasn't working, and there didn't seem to be an exit ramp.

The New Jersey Turnpike of my career was one gray potholed lane after another with smokestacks in the background. I had no idea that New Jersey was actually a green beautiful place somewhere beyond the periphery of the prescribed path. Once I took the exit ramp, a whole new New Jersey opened up to me.

FOUNDATIONAL MYTHS

Figuring out what I stood for was important, but putting my values into action meant challenging the foundational myths I thought were core to my being.

What were the myths I told myself? I didn't have any good ideas. I couldn't be a CEO because I didn't know how to code. I wasn't technical.

That meant that despite working on companies for 20 years, and having strong opinions about how to build them, I'd removed a specific, lucrative, and fulfilling possibility for myself immediately. As the CEO of Pavilion, it's clear now how wrong I was.

Why do we tell ourselves such myths?

Fear. Fear is the underpinning of so much of what we believe in life and what we tell ourselves is possible. Fear is about the unknown. Fear is about thinking something might be tragic or terrible or have some horrible outcome.

I was held rigidly in place by fear. Part of it was a lack of experience. Part of it was frivolous spending and a strange relationship with money, living under debt and constantly comparing myself to such an extent that every dollar I had was really about propping up my identity.

On that trip to Italy, Camille and I first visited a friend of her late mother, Marco Musso, in the city of Genoa. We then rented a car and drove down the coast to a beautiful old hotel called La Poste Vecchia, built on ancient Roman ruins. The trip was off to an amazing start. It seemed like one of those trips and one of those places that inspires you. Maybe things would be different.

But then things turned as we continued on to the Amalfi Coast. We were driving down beautiful winding mountain roads into the towns of Sorrento and Positano. This area of the world is supposed to be some of the most beautiful in existence and I was prepared for some kind of transformational, transporting experience.

We arrived at our hotel, and everything immediately started to feel less than perfect. I do have a tendency to find fault, and doubt started creeping in. There were ants on the pillows. I thought, doesn't this place seem a little shabby for $500 per night? It was the most I'd ever spent on a hotel room to that point. Shouldn't it be the most amazing experience?

These types of fancy European-style places can be toxic if you don't have the right mindset or the right resources. On that trip, I felt like the meter was always running. Every cocktail, every bottle of water pushing me backwards against the wall and creating more and more stress as I tabulated bills and invoices in my head. I spent countless hours counting and recounting the money in my accounts against my credit card debt and sinking deeper and deeper into black darkness.

Fear. Fear wrapped itself around me like an anaconda on that trip. I carried this fear and stress and anxiety with me for years—and still do if I don't force myself to reset. There is still an active sense of dread lurking inside my head. A sense that something is wrong.

For so many years, I didn't understand that dread. Because when it wells up inside you, your brain takes it in and puts words against it. It's all-consuming. You feel like the choices you make are predetermined by those feelings, so your brain takes dread and fear and spins it into stories. Those stories are arbitrary, but at the time you don't know it.

One story I told myself: I didn't deserve this Italian vacation. Another story: whether I deserved it or not, I couldn't afford it. The dread loved my money anxieties. Fed off of them, always wanting more. I spiraled down, down, down.

The dread led me to visions of the IRS and a feeling of being trapped, tied down, always constrained by earthly limitations, squeezed too tightly.

In fact, the dread loved to take those money fears, remove my personal agency, and then paste them unfairly onto other people.

Other people were the problem. I told myself outside pressures were putting me in a position that forced my back against the wall. With each passing minute, my anxiety would grow and compound—and grow and compound.

These are hard things to "fix." There actually isn't much fixing of them because there is some kernel of truth to all of them. Of course, your fear and dread know that—that's why they're so powerful.

So maybe my dread would have been lessened if we had never taken a vacation. But maybe I was using all of these stories about vacation and spending as a means of displacing my own insecurities.

Figuring out who you want to be in life is hard. I felt completely trapped in 2017. But the beginnings of my personal and spiritual transformation finally took hold when I decided it was time to take the exit ramp and reset my destination.

RESETTING IS A PROCESS, NOT AN ACT

When I was fired for the penultimate time, there was of course fear and trepidation. Those foundational myths were potent. But there was also an awakening, one that unfolded over a period of years once I decided to take control of my life.

From fear or exhaustion or whatever process you want to call it, there was a beginning. That process of resetting can be construed as a lowering of expectations, but that's not how I experienced it.

There was no need involved. Perhaps that was the secret. There was no desperation. The motivation came from a place of energy and enthusiasm and fulfillment, instead of a desperate anxiety to fit myself into other conceptions or definitions.

I wrote down everything I knew and began to imagine my life differently—not as an act of rebellion, but as a complete redefinition.

I looked inward and tried simply to place independence and autonomy at the center and then layer-in all the work I had done with Jim Rosen on establishing my values. My life's success moved away from a simple definition of net worth to something more modest and much more empowering.

Once you realize you can make money on your own, doing the thing that you love doing, then perhaps that is wealth in and of itself. Wealth is really about the freedom and independence to pursue your passions and your ability to first and foremost prioritize your own time and energy. Those things don't require a certain amount of money, although they do require some of it.

A Sense of Becoming

By December 2017, my consulting business was up and running. After my first consulting gig with LeagueApps, I consulted with a company called Optimove that provided software to retailers. Then, I consulted with a company called WayUp that provided a platform for college graduates to find their first job. It finally seemed that I was headed in the right direction.

But the thing I remember most about that time was taking an entirely different kind of trip with Camille and our beautiful dog, Walter, to California.

We stayed at a house in Laguna Niguel, up the hill from Laguna Beach. I had taken this trip without a steady job, but with the knowledge that I had a pipeline full of consulting clients waiting for me when I returned.

And unlike the trip to Italy the summer before, this felt entirely manageable. And I felt free. For the first time in as long as I can remember, I didn't have anyone to answer to back on the East Coast.

Camille and I would wake up every day and go for a hike in the trails around Laguna. We'd eat a late lunch and go sit on the beach with Walter and film short videos where his fluffy coat would blow in the breeze. We rented a Ford Mustang convertible and Walty would get in and hop into the passenger seat and then we'd drive to pick up some green juice for Camille while she slept, and we'd listen to "Money for Nothing" by the Dire Straits very loud while we basked in the sunshine and the wind in our respective hair and fluffy fur coat.

But the best feeling was simply a soft, warm exhilaration when I realized I was on a path to doing something that truly aligned with what I stood for. It was almost like my sails had caught the solar winds of the universe. My toes dug into the sand in Laguna, on a blanket next to my wife and dog, and I was thinking that the future only contained possibility. That somehow I had wrested my independence and control of my life from others and given it back to myself. I finally had a new destination on the horizon.

CHAPTER 3 TACTICS: BUILD YOUR "ABOUT YOU" DECK

When Camille told me to write down everything I knew about building a business, she was intuitive and prescient on a practice that can help change your career and enable your success. Which is a simple thing—document your expertise and the concepts you develop over time.

Keep a Google Doc of notes, strategies, and tactics you have accumulated over time and over the course of your career and your work. Jot down key insights. The document can evolve in any number of ways, but as you grow you'll slowly build your own playbook.

Once you have a batch of notes and ideas and have refined them, this can become part of your brand, resume, and toolkit. When you interview for opportunities, you'll be differentiated because you'll have a ready-made overview of how you operate and what you put into practice.

Additionally, over the years, I've also compiled an "About Sam" document that I share with incoming employees. This goes into my mood, temperament, how I like to receive feedback, and how I operate. It helps manage expectations appropriately and directly addresses the years of feedback I've received on how I process my emotions.

As much as I'd love to be more consistent as an executive, the reality is that I've always been a bit up and down. But as Anne Juceam told me, self-awareness is kindness.

If I can prepare people for what it's like to work with me and, as an executive, can outline my beliefs on operations, strategy, and tactics, I can demonstrate that I've been using the years of my career to intentionally lean into key experiences and challenges.

The process of documentation helps clarify your beliefs and practices while also enhancing the perception that you are a student of the game and take the time to develop actual frameworks.

CHAPTER 4

Powered by Generosity

I'd been convening people for years. Even in my personal life, I'd always been the one organizing Guys Weekend every summer where we'd all go rent a house in the woods for a long weekend and hang out and laugh and grill and drink and play cards.

Gathering others and facilitating discussions became a superpower of mine. The awkward silences and grasping for conversation that usually accompanies networking events make my skin crawl. I hated the mindless chitchat that never really seemed to serve a purpose. Traditional networking always felt like you were just collecting a list of names for clout. I wanted to find points of true connection with others. To see where I could help them out or help them solve a challenge.

That is what still fuels me to this day. Helping others succeed is core to my being. It is my reason for being.

THE ORIGINS OF GENEROSITY

I don't remember when I first struck upon the idea that doing something for someone else and not needing anything in return felt so good. At some point between my time at Axial and when the business of Pavilion fully emerged, I had hit on this very simple concept.

Perhaps it's because it's such a challenge—like trying to unlock a very specific kind of puzzle piece. Maybe it was from my years spent at Gerson Lehrman Group, an expert networking company that was effectively about matchmaking. Maybe it was my Jewish roots—perhaps some part of my DNA was a yenta in Poland trying to find exactly the right combination between a man and a woman.

But for whatever reason, I started to discover how much I liked doing things for other people. And specifically, as I think about it, not just doing things, but connecting them to specific people. And I especially liked it when I didn't need anything in return nor want anything in return.

There was a certain power, a certain liberation, in only issuing IOUs into the universe. There was a freedom, an exhilarating freedom, in not keeping score. It somehow gave me power and confidence and enthusiasm. Because I was willing to "leave money on the table."

Specifically, I loved, and still love, matchmaking. It's like a puzzle. Who are just the right two people who can be put together with sufficient context to yield something useful. The thrill is in understanding that you don't necessarily need to make a perfect match. The universe, mutual energy, people's interest and willingness in pursuing something novel and exciting, that will be the plaster of paris and Silly Putty that sticks the relationship together.

So it needn't be perfect. And, in fact, it becomes more beautiful when it's not something you expected at all. You introduce someone in food technology to a marketer, and pretty soon they're starting a company together. You introduce someone you worked with years ago to someone else that seems like a fit for their personality, and pretty soon, one of them has a new job.

It's a legitimate thrill.

And, again, it's even more thrilling when you don't ask for anything.

That's because everyone asks for something.

BE BIG, DON'T BE SMALL

Everyone asks for something. Everyone.

Everyone is common. Being common is so common. Someone does something for you, they immediately have their hand out. "Lemme hold something." Someone makes an introduction for you, let's talk referral fee. Someone wants your help hiring for a position, gimme that placement fee. Someone wants to share an idea, sign that NDA, there's only one of these beautiful ideas, and I can't risk you stealing it.

That's small.

There's a scene in *Fargo* where Steve Buscemi's character Carl Showalter decided not to park in the parking garage. He was only there for a few minutes but the parking attendant insists on making sure he pays. The sign said nonrefundable. Buscemi says, "These are the limits of your life, pal."

And it's a joke, because if anyone is trapped it's Carl Showalter. But the phrase has always stuck with me.

People who chisel you. People who needle you on every last point. People who put in a nondisparagement clause but don't make it mutual. People who need you to ask to make everything reciprocal in a boilerplate agreement. These people are small people.

Big people understand the great arithmetic of the universe. Big people understand that fullness and vision and expansiveness all comes back to you in the end. Generous people tip 40%, even 50% sometimes. They understand that there are ripples to surprising people on the upside. There are ripples in the universe that spread across the energy fabric of humanity when you do good things and do them out of sheer joy, do them because the joy itself is the very real compensation. And, to be candid, a slightly less noble emotion, the pride. The pride in not asking. The feeling of completeness you get when you don't need anything from anyone else. You do it for the abundance.

That's the beauty and the power of generosity. It fills you up. It's a belief system. It's a belief system in a place that you already are.

My friends and I first started getting together for dinners at a sushi place around the corner from where I worked at Axial. We'd stay in touch between dinners over email with everyone on the CC: line. Eventually, I created a Google Group and gave it a name—the New York Revenue Collective.

Long before my rest stop realization, I brought together this collective of people who all believed that we could achieve more by helping one another. At the time, the average tenure of a chief revenue officer (CRO) was 18 months. My friends and I were in high-growth, high-stress roles, and the only way for us to get through it was together.

I facilitated the dinners and the emails, moderating the conversation to ensure everyone was gaining real value from our gatherings. It became a place where we could ask questions in confidence, talk about the tough challenges of our roles, and bounce ideas off each other.

You see, the more senior your role, the fewer peers you have within your organization. It can often be a lonely place, without colleagues who understand the decisions you need to make and the weight placed on your shoulders. The New York Revenue Collective became the outlet we all needed. And it was built on the simple premises of mutual support and kindness. What I call "give to get." A new kind of community powered by generosity.

I began charging dues for Revenue Collective on January 1, 2018, and I sold a sponsorship to Salesloft for $10,000.

All of a sudden, I had a real business. The germination of a business, yes, but a business nonetheless. One I had started myself and that was built on the characteristics that I valued. Alongside my growing consulting business, I was stepping into the career I had always wanted. And I was building this business, building this community in a new way.

BUILDING A NEW KIND OF COMMUNITY

It was a strange moment. Most communities were, and still are, free. But I decided to test a hypothesis—people will pay if there was enough value in it for them. The Revenue Collective initially charged just $50 a month. Not a lot, but enough to see if there was something worthwhile there. Out of the 22 people in the New York Revenue Collective, 20 decided to pay—the first being my good friend Michael Manne, currently the CRO of Ocrolus.

As I found out in my work with my coach, Jim Rosen, I stood for helping people I care about and respect to achieve their goals. So, the New York Revenue Collective was predicated on a simple idea: I would do as much as I could to help people in their careers. I would help them find jobs. I would share compensation information with them. I would bring in experts and teachers. And I would create a sense of community.

But I never wanted to create a community just for its own sake. I wanted a community built on values that taught people that being generous and helpful could pay dividends over the long term.

We established simple ground rules—no spamming or direct solicitation. The flip side was you had to be courteous and responsive to your fellow Members. We believed in a world of "give to get," where before asking for a favor, you first tried to do someone else a favor.

By this point, I was sick of business being cutthroat. I knew we could all win if we supported each other. So I made this a foundational aspect of my community. In exchange for your dues, we all will do everything in our power to help you. It might not seem like it, but this is actually radically different to how most communities are structured.

THE PROBLEM WITH MOST COMMUNITIES

Because most communities are free, the only way to make money from them is to sell sponsorships, essentially selling access to the community to other people. Inevitably that means that Members of the community become the product. And that product is predicated on size—you need as many email addresses as possible to sell to sponsors for the community to be effective. Which means you need to lower your entrance criteria, letting more and more people into the community. The end result is inevitably noise.

And underneath that noise there are two fundamentally broken assumptions—that the community itself wasn't worth paying for directly and that people should be exploited for the act of convening.

We challenged both of those assumptions in the New York Revenue Collective, and still do today in Pavilion.

That's not to say that growing membership is a bad thing for a community. It's my dream that one day there will be hundreds of thousands, maybe even millions, of Pavilion Members around the world who operate on a shared set of values.

But because we accept money from our Members, we are beholden to them. Our incentives as a business are completely aligned with our Members, our customers. It is regulated capitalism at its finest. We only make money if people value what we do. If we stop providing value to our Members, they stop paying us. It's honestly kind of beautiful in its simplicity.

The reason I took the sponsorship money from Salesloft, and the reason we accepted $25 million in funding from Elephant Ventures in 2021, was so that I could build bigger and more valuable programs for the Members. In 2018, I used the dues and sponsorship money to build the New York Revenue Collective into a truly valuable community, not just a dinner club for venting. That capital allowed us to bring in speakers, to make more connections, and ultimately get people the resources they needed to keep climbing that corporate ladder.

In 2021, we were operating at a profit. We didn't need the investment, but our goal that year was to bring as much value to the membership as possible.

We heard time and time again from our community Members that you don't learn how to be an executive in school. So we used that money to build out learning programs that did teach people how to be successful executives. We used that money to build the structures needed for a global community to scale and continue providing value.

Bloating your membership for the sake of selling sponsorships is a pitfall of short-term, transactional thinking. It's not sustainable, and in the end your community becomes diluted. The reason people joined the community in the first place becomes less important than meeting the demands of your sponsors or advertisers.

You end up monetizing every other aspect of the community to maintain its status as free. But it's not free. That membership comes at the expense of your personal data. Your clout. Your right to live a life free of spam and ads. You become a lead. Fish in a barrel for headhunters. You become the product.

The free community business model is inherently flawed. But, it's not the only problem with most communities.

So many communities do not know what they stand for. They don't know why they exist. Think about the professional communities you and colleagues belong to. What do they stand for? What is their mission?

So many communities articulate abstractions because they're not quite sure. They'll say things like "we exist to elevate the profession of sales." Okay. What does that actually mean?

Elevate the profession, how? Elevate it, why? What this signals to me is a group of people got together and thought they should form a group, and didn't think about much else. It ties right back to the short-term thinking of making a community free. Both are short-term answers to a problem, not a long-term solution.

At Pavilion, we exist to help our Members achieve their professional potential. Our goal is broad enough that it doesn't limit what we can do for our Members, but actionable enough to tell people why they should join. If you have career goals, if you think you haven't reached your potential in the workplace, we can help you. How we help takes myriad forms, but you know that when you join Pavilion, we will do everything in our power to make your career aspirations possible.

If you join a community whose mission is to "elevate the profession," how does that help you? Will you be better at your job if the industry was more respected? Does being respected mean you operate on a set of core values? Does this community exist to give back to its Members?

When I was at Axial between 2010 and 2015, I had access to a community platform run by First Round Capital, who invested in us. People would share articles and they would help each other and answer questions.

When I was fired from Axial, I was barred from everything. Logged out and locked out of every account I had, including the community platform. That community only existed to help employees of First Round Capital companies, and I was no longer one of them.

Not only had I lost my job, but I lost many of the connections and mentorship that would have helped me grow into a stronger leader. They tossed me out because I was no longer of use to them.

What it comes down to is this: that community did not serve its Members. It served investors and CEOs. The actual day-to-day Members meant little to them. They could be easily replaced.

Every community I had been a part of, up until Revenue Collective and Pavilion, was too scared to build something that didn't ultimately serve investors or didn't ultimately serve CEOs. From the beginning, Pavilion was built by operators. We wanted to build a safe place for them to talk about the challenges of their roles, where they didn't need to worry about what they said getting back to the C-suite.

For most of our existence, we didn't even let CEOs join. Beginning in 2021, we started building curated cohorts of CEOs, letting in limited numbers at a time and building a new part of the community. This initiative was led by several existing Members who had been promoted to C-level roles.

But overwhelmingly, our membership continues to be operators, and they continue to drive how we operate. With the majority of our funding coming from these kinds of Members, we will continue to do what they ask us to.

The secret to building a community, or a business, really is simple. Listen to what people want and give it to them. Give it to them because you genuinely want to help them. When you love and serve your customers generously, the growth possibilities are endless.

LOVE FOR CUSTOMERS: THE MISSING PIECE OF THE EQUATION

The notion of truly loving and respecting your customers took hold of me while I was working for a company that did the exact opposite.

Technologically, the company had everything going for it. But they came to believe that they were smarter than the customer, going as far as to have open disdain for customers.

Unit economics are crucial in judging the performance of a business, but retaining those customers is just as important. Customers talk, and negative experiences tend to have more power than positive ones. If your organization has a reputation of being hard to work with, that is not a notion easily overcome.

The truth is that great products are built by people who love their customers. If you put generosity at the heart of your business and truly listen to your customers, you'll probably end up building something meaningful and compelling to them. And you'll be a company they actually want to do business with.

Listening to your customers is so often overlooked in business. We have a tendency to overcomplicate and think we know best. But our customers know best. They will tell you what they need. All you have to do is listen, and then act on the things that are within your control.

This is why we end every week at Pavilion with Member success stories. They help the team remember who we are here for and motivate them to go into the next week serving the people who make our company possible. Without our Members, there would be no Pavilion.

We created learning and training opportunities because our Members told us they needed them. We formed small councils within Pavilion because our Members told us they wanted more intimate interactions and connections. We created a group dedicated to helping Members find their next opportunity when they lost jobs due to the pandemic. None of these initiatives were my idea. They all came from our membership, who pay us dues to make it happen.

Of course you need to be strategic with your business and decide which feedback to act on. But if you ever feel unsure about your direction, listen to your customers with an open mind. They'll tell you where to go.

GENEROSITY CAN BE A COMPETITIVE ADVANTAGE

What this all comes down to is that a business built on generosity will bring back everything (and more) that it puts out into the universe.

When I said Pavilion was founded on "give to get," this is why. Generosity and giving before you get is not simple altruism. It is a sound business philosophy that can change your relationship to those around you and help you accumulate influence and power.

We have been taught in business and in life not to leave anything on the table. To never split the difference. To always get more out of an interaction than you give.

I'm here to tell you that this is ultimately a destructive and short-sighted way to live. Inevitably, someone will come along who is more cutthroat, more reckless, and more willing to squeeze out every last drop. Then what will you be left with? A string of pissed off acquaintances who will do nothing to help you get back on your feet? A list of regrets? Maybe some money?

I used to live in that scarcity mindset. That if I didn't take, someone else would. By the time I was standing on the beach in California, after I'd had that epiphany on the New Jersey Turnpike, I could see how wrong I was. It was only when I gave to others that I truly started to gain.

And it's not about being selfless or that I'm less greedy. What it is about is being okay without instant gratification. It's about knowing that what you do now will pay back in dividends in the future. It's about being long-term greedy.

Being generous doesn't mean you don't want power or wealth or notoriety. Being generous is a long-term competitive advantage that will build all of those things over time.

Generous people accumulate power because, by consistently looking to help other people, you become, de facto, someone who can help other people. Being someone who can help other people is powerful and soon, simply through the act of serving others honestly and without expectation, more and more people come to you for assistance, and they will come back to you with a variety of opportunities. The results compound.

So many short-term thinkers only see the table in front of them. But there's a bigger table with more money if you think about your life and your career in the long term.

If I had tried to turn the Pavilion into a recruiting firm or if I had tried to start an investment fund right out of the gate, I wouldn't be anywhere close to where I am now.

The Pavilion business model is a much, much bigger idea than starting an executive search firm. It's an idea powered by generosity, loving our Members, and bringing them value. That idea took us to a $100 million valuation, and will take us as far as we want to go.

Generosity can take you where you want to go, too.

PUTTING GENEROSITY INTO PRACTICE

So how do you put generosity at the center of your business?

Look for ways to help people every day.

Introduce a colleague to someone else in your network. Look over a friend's résumé. Recommend a book or a program you know will help someone further their career. Offer advice on a difficult work situation. Make connections. And ask for nothing in return.

We charged a flat fee. Most communities will tell you there's a playbook to monetization. You start a job board and charge for it. You sell sponsorships. You start a recruiting business and charge for it.

Pavilion is able to fundamentally differentiate itself by not doing those things. Instead, we charge one flat fee and try to pour as much value as we can into it. The price you join at is the price you pay as long as you want to remain a Member. We still have original Members paying $50 a year.

We believed and continue to believe in the fundamental long-term value of customers that come back again and again because they know they'll be treated fairly and with kindness, and we are happy to create much more value than we ever capture in the form of dollars.

This long-term focus—putting trust and generosity into the core of what we do—creates a far more powerful beacon for those in desperate search of like-minded travelers, rather than nickel and diming them for each and every service we provide.

Members trust us because they know we're working for them. My peers trusted me because I led with generosity and didn't ask for anything in return. And when I needed their support, they were thrilled to lend it to me. At the time I had no idea if or when I would need to cash in, but when I did, the generosity came back to me tenfold.

Make generosity your competitive advantage. Believe in the long term. Believe in a world where others are also living by the same lessons. Accept the fact that it won't be everyone, but also accept that there will be enough positive energy created by your generosity that you'll achieve what you want to achieve and you'll do so with a full heart.

When you build something on a set of core values, fuel it with generosity, and practice sound business strategies for long-term growth, you'll be able to capitalize on more opportunities than most.

CHAPTER 4 TACTICS: FIND SOMEONE TO HELP

I don't like networking. I don't like happy hours. I do like helping people. So many times people ask me in career conversations what the key is to career advancement. I typically say the same thing, "Look for someone to help."

Helping can take a lot of forms, but the easiest way to help is to connect people based on mutual interests. And not mutual interests in the sense that they both like rock music. But mutual interests in that one person has a need and one person has a capability.

This typically manifests itself into job placement. Someone looking for a great VP of marketing coupled with someone who is a great marketer. By cataloging discussions either intentionally through a notebook or document or just by remembering, you can find ways to create matches between people.

Do this consistently over time and do not ask for a finder's fee or any kind of money. Just focus on accumulating the experience of making useful connections and then differentiate yourself by not seeking immediate reward for your efforts.

And don't worry that you're not getting paid to foster this assistance. You are getting paid. You are getting paid based on the increase to your reputation, the increase to your visibility, and the cumulative likelihood that over time people will remember your assistance and contributions and will find some way to return the favor.

CHAPTER 5

The Next Right Step

One of the reasons people find long-term thinking challenging is that they don't know what to do now to make that long-term plan possible. It can seem abstract and overwhelming to always have your sights set on the horizon. While you may know deep down something will pay off in the future, how do you pay your bills today?

I get it. Instant gratification is so ingrained in our culture, it's hard to see another way. But playing the long game doesn't mean you do nothing in the short term. All you need to do is take the next right step.

There are lots of heads of strategy out there. And it's true that some business decisions are incredibly complicated.

But fundamentally business, as with life, is not about having a specific plan for every eventuality but having a set of principles and values and then taking the appropriate next step when presented.

My original goal for Revenue Collective was 2,000 total Members by the end of 2020. Instead, at the end of 2020, we had close to 4,000 Members.

In 2016, we were effectively an email group with quarterly dinners. In 2019 we became a dinner group with a vibrant Slack community. In 2020, when we grew fivefold during a global pandemic, we began programming over 25 digital events every single week. In 2021, we rebranded to Pavilion and opened the doors to more than 7,000 Members.

This is not because I'm a genius. This is because we used core values to inform our decision making and leveraged a rough plan. We then took the logical next right step.

It's likely true that as a public company executive you need far more foresight than when you are starting a tiny little startup. But my experience has always been that if you just take the next logical step, do the next right thing, you don't necessarily have to worry too much about where you'll be in two years or three years.

Of course it's nice to have an idea of where you want to head, and you need a plan to help ground your vision.

But as I always like to say, "The future always arrives right on time." Somehow or someway, things that seem hazy, distant, or impossible out into the distance become clearer as the time gets closer.

There's the old adage that the journey of a thousand miles begins with a single step. And then the next and then the next.

MAKING OUR FIRST HIRE

In 2018, Revenue Collective was gaining steam. I had taken one last job at a startup that unfortunately ended up being the opposite of everything we're talking about in this book. But with the severance I negotiated, I had the seed money to take Revenue Collective full time. I was ready to take that step.

But to take that step, I knew I needed help. I remembered a woman I had been in contact with over the years—a Penn grad, lawyer, and mother of two looking to re-enter the workforce. Her name was Anne Juceam.

We had had a breakfast months prior as she was looking to take her interests and capabilities as an operator and entrepreneur and join up with some kind of exciting opportunity. I'd made a bunch of introductions for her, but none of them panned out. But her name popped into my head, and I thought, "Maybe Anne is available to help."

I emailed her in October, and she helped me put together a Christmas party for the Revenue Collective featuring Manny Medina, the CEO of Outreach. She became the first employee of Revenue Collective and is still with us today as our VP of People after building and running our operations function for the first three years of her tenure.

Together we built Revenue Collective's first pipeline and established an onboarding sequence, training our Members on how we operate. We started seeing 15, 20, 50 applications roll in every week. We interviewed every prospective Member ourselves. We did every job, just the two of us.

With a long-term vision guiding us, we were able to make day-to-day decisions that would serve our plan. By taking it one step at a time, we made huge strides.

Around the same time, my friend Max Altschuler asked me to host a podcast for his community, Sales Hacker. I used the Sales Hacker Podcast as a springboard for Revenue Collective, mentioning it during episodes and outlining our core beliefs. Sales Hacker had a mailing list upwards of 100,000 people, and soon there were people emailing me from far-flung places like London and Amsterdam and Toronto asking to set up chapters based on the ideas I'd been talking about on the podcast.

I hadn't anticipated the word spreading so quickly, but when those people reached out, I took the calls, and happily agreed.

Traditionally if you're scaling a business, you think of the big markets first—New York, San Francisco, Chicago. But our growth came from people raising their hand, saying they, too, believed in a different type of world.

So when opportunities presented themselves in smaller markets, we took them, knowing we had a passionate base to build off of. London was our second chapter, spearheaded by Tom Glason. Next, we gained a following in Boston, Toronto, Amsterdam, Atlanta, and Indianapolis. Instead of forcing ourselves into a market, we listened to our Members and built chapters where they lived, where they operated businesses.

This wasn't what we would have put in a business plan, but it led to faster and further growth than I could have ever imagined. As I'm writing this book, we now have more than 50 chapters worldwide, stretching from Singapore to Copenhagen to Brazil. But our operating model remains largely unchanged. When a group of people who are passionate about our community and ideals comes forward, we give them as many resources as we can to help them succeed. We listen to what they need and give it to them, to the best of our ability. We see where they are headed and make strides toward that future. It really doesn't need to be more complicated than that.

When you build a business with values and generosity as your guide, you will always have a framework to move you forward. The decisions you make from day to day might change, you might have many, many short-term goals along the way, but your North Star remains true.

Working on Revenue Collective full time changed everything for me. I could finally see that I just wasn't wired to work on someone else's dream. All of my best ideas belonged solely to me, and I could make them happen if I wanted to. I finally felt free.

During this time, Camille and I spent three months living in Austin, Texas. I was running more. I was setting my own calendar. I was finally stepping into my own. The best parts of me were beginning to shine. Not that I still didn't have challenges or bumps in the road, but it really felt like a weight had been lifted off my shoulders. The clouds cleared enough for me to see the horizon. And I could take one step, then another, and soon I would be running into a future I had only dreamed existed.

The point of this book isn't to say you need to start a business to feel this way. But, if you find something that you believe in with your whole being, you should pull that thread.

PULLING THE THREAD

I often say that the future arrives right on time. So many people spend a lot of time mapping out a far-flung strategy. And it's certainly true that you need to have some kind of vision for the future.

My personal vision has always been specific in the near term and less specific the further out you go. Sounds straightforward, but I feel like sometimes people feel this innate sense of terror that they don't know exactly what their company might look like in two years and that's a huge problem.

But, especially in the early days, businesses are a lot like the Sweater Song by Weezer. If you simply take the next right step, if you just keep pulling the thread, you will seldom go wrong. Which just means, don't worry too much about two years from now. Worry about now. Worry about making sure that you do the next thing on your to-do list.

Eventually over time it accumulates, and you can take stock of your progress and momentum after a period of months and years, knowing that most of the time, the journey itself was keeping the end roughly in mind but staring pretty intently at the next decision that you had to make.

As I was working with Anne and living in Austin, I knew that for me the next right step was making Revenue Collective a true value-based organization and codifying some of these principles based on the experience I'd gained over the preceding 20 years.

MAPPING YOUR CORE VALUES INTO DECISION MAKING

From my coaching sessions with Jim Rosen, I knew that I stood for helping people I care about and respect achieve their goals, and I wanted to build a space powered by generosity. But as Revenue Collective grew, we needed more detailed principles that would guide our decision making.

Most companies get this wrong. So often, businesses have generic "values" they plaster up on the wall or on the website that have no real meaning. Values and what you stand for are only useful if they're specific and if they invoke a choice. Saying one of your values is "Breathing oxygen" is not meaningful since we all need oxygen to live.

Values need to mean something to your business. Values should help you make decisions. Values should train people how to operate within your business and the expectations you have for them. Values should be the framework for doing business.

My friend Dan Pink says there are three things that drive motivation: autonomy, mastery, and purpose. Everybody wants to know the context, the purpose in which they operate. Values provide that context. They give people the guardrails with which to make decisions and to know they are on the right path. My personal exploration of values discussed in Chapter 3 directly influenced the organizational values of Pavilion. I wanted my business to stand for what I stood for. Even if you aren't starting your own business, look for one whose values align with your own.

I always say to my team that if you don't know what to do today, find someone to help. That is the essence of all of our values. But by providing more nuanced context, we can help guide everyone on the team to make decisions that align with our long-term vision and uphold our promises to our Members.

Values + Strategy = Autonomy

To the point of motivation, and to the point of leverage, I find the combination of a well-communicated plan (Strategy) coupled with a clear and reinforced set of values to be the thing that enables autonomy within an organization.

Imagine you need to cross a thick forest and arrive at a specific place at a specific time on the other side of the woods. Values are the rules you will use as you move through the woods (e.g., don't eat those berries, only sleep in trees, don't harm the bears), and the strategy is the map, compass, and supplies you'll carry with you.

With those two things, you should be able to navigate safely across. And your manager or executive won't have had to make sure they were present for every single decision. And that is leverage.

Leverage can only be created when you arm your team with the necessary information and tools they need to do their jobs and then give them the decision-making framework to tackle difficult problems through the values you instill.

Values Should Help Decision Making

Importantly, as you think about the values you want for your organization or the things that motivate you and define who you are, I would offer the idea that values are only useful if they assist with decision making. I often joke that it's not useful to have a value like "We believe in breathing oxygen" because as humans we don't really have a choice in the matter. We either do or we die.

So it's useful to build in specific-enough values that have enough of the essence of who we are that they actually help you make specific discrete binary decisions.

The set of values we have at Pavilion are:

- Members first
- We get by giving
- We deliver X+Y
- Listen closely, act quickly
- Diversity makes us better
- We deliver results
- We choose to come from kindness

Members First

We work backwards from our Members' success. That's our first principle. We don't solve for internal politics or what's easier for us. We solve first and foremost for our Members. We go to great lengths to help our Members. We do things that aren't scalable.

We take their calls on a Saturday. We offer time we didn't know we had. This is about them. Not us. Helping them.

Members First is not just a trope for its own sake. It explicitly speaks to decisions we need to make internally.

If we are focused on our Members, who are not our users, but rather our customers, then we can decide if the decision we're taking is better for us or for them. As a company scales, there is a need to drive efficiency, but that efficiency often comes at the cost of customer experience. Think of the algorithm of your favorite social media platform. Algorithms are good for business. Companies will pay a lot of money to be served up to a relevant audience. That's when you, the user, become the product, as we discussed in the previous chapter.

So even though you call for a chronological timeline or other features that would make your user experience better, the company doubles down on the algorithm and advertising dollars. Because it is better for them. Again, I'm not saying this is necessarily nefarious on their part, but it is how most companies operate. It is a strategic point of difference to put the end user first.

When at the crossroads of *easy for us* or *better for our Members*, we do our best at Pavilion to make a decision that errs on the side of the Members, not our internal needs.

For example, we call our Members the moment they sign up to join Pavilion. At the time we made that decision, we didn't have any infrastructure to make phone calls at all. We knew making this decision would involve retraining our Member Success Team and take up hours of their time every week. But we firmly believed it would improve our Member happiness, result in a better onboarding experience for them, and ultimately drive our Net Promoter Score higher.

Members First is our North Star and most important value. As you'll see below, our values and the way we operate have evolved over time, getting clearer and more specific to help employees make decisions. However, the value that will never change is Members First.

When you are building a business or helping to drive a culture of kindness, you must have at least one central tenet that remains true no matter what. A beacon that will always shine and guide the way for your team. When your business inevitably becomes more complicated and nuanced and layered, there will still be that source of truth you can turn to that will keep you on the path you intended.

We Get by Giving

Giving and helping are their own reward. We are playing a longer game. Our relationships aren't transactional. We believe and know that through helping others we will help ourselves in ways that will be far greater and more impactful than we ever imagined. We know the world is not zero sum. Our help to others increases its abundance.

"We Get by Giving" is a central theme of this book—and crucial to how we operate at Pavilion. We wrote this philosophy into our core values because we believe that reciprocity and kindness will fundamentally change the business world. And if you've made it this far, I hope you believe that, too.

In Chapter 4, we covered how generosity can be a competitive advantage in business. It's not altruistic to put others first in the sense that it is a sacrifice for you. It is a long-term strategy where everything you give will come back to you in abundance because you have the patience to play the long game.

Just as "Members First" means we sometimes take inefficient routes, "We Get by Giving" means that the ripples we create by helping others are far, far greater than a one-time, immediate payoff.

We Deliver X+Y

Doing the bare minimum (X) is never acceptable. We ask ourselves, "Why are we doing this?" and anticipate not just the minimum requirements (X) but the added requirements (Y) even if they weren't requested. We don't just identify problems (X). We identify problems and suggest solutions (X+Y). We take pride in moving outside our job description and outside our comfort zone. We get our hands dirty. We pick up the phone. We take action to drive the business forward and help our Members thrive. We deliver X+Y.

The concept of X+Y came from my first job out of college—the one I left to start that ill-fated record label. My boss Omid C. Tofigh at Stern Stewart called me into his office for a performance review. I strolled in thinking I was about to be praised for a job well done. I was hitting all of the metrics I was told to. I did everything by the book.

What Omid told me crushed me—he was underwhelmed by my work. I sank down. How could that be true? I came into the office every day, did my work, and delivered the intended results. Didn't I?

He told me that I only delivered X. Exactly what I was told to do and no further. I wasn't thinking about ways to improve, to drive more, to push further. I was coasting, doing just fine and nothing further.

He told me if I had ambitions, if I wanted to be more, I needed to start thinking about how I can go beyond X. How I can add Y.

There's that long-term thinking again. Those who need that instant gratification, who can only see what is in front of them, shoot for X. Those who understand that there is always more you can be doing look not just for one outcome or solution, but a long-term plan to deliver better results. That's X+Y—yet another differentiating factor for your business.

Much later, a friend told me that numbers-missers tend to stay numbers-missers. They come up with excuses instead of solutions. But numbers-beaters tend to remain numbers-beaters, always pushing to add Y.

Both of these stories took hold of me. I wanted to create a culture of X+Y, of numbers-beaters. I wanted my team to know that to make this the best business it can be, to truly serve our Members, and to keep giving, we can't just deliver minimum expectations. We all need to anticipate needs, use our brains, and take pride in our work. The results will be a company of doers who delight customers and make the business better every day.

When you are outlining values for your business, think about the kind of company you want. Do you want to build a place where people clock in and clock out with little thought in between? Or do you want a company where your people are innovative, pushing the boundaries of what's possible? If it's the latter, you need to create that framework through your values and build it into everything you do.

Listen Closely, Act Quickly

Our Members will tell us what we need to build if we listen. But we must listen to them. This means careful observation and empathy. This means that we talk less than they do. And once we absorb an idea, we move very quickly to execute it. Speed becomes a competitive advantage unto itself. The modern world requires rapid iteration and tolerates a lower degree of perfection in favor of speed and responsiveness. We know that. We use that to our advantage. We listen closely. We act quickly.

We'll explore this concept in more detail in the next chapter, but what this value tells Pavilion employees is that progress is better than perfection. Tying back to Members First and loving your customer, our Members tell us what they need. Your customers will tell you what you need. It is then your job to make it happen.

An extension of the next right step—Listen Closely, Act Quickly—means that you don't need a 10-year plan to execute on something you know to be true. Take in the information from your customers, identify patterns in feedback, and take action based on that feedback.

I know it can be easy to fall into a feedback spiral. One person says they love something about your product. The next says they hate that same thing. The conflicting statements cause you to gather more and more and more information before you act. Then you end up not acting at all.

Of course you can't make everyone happy. You can do everything your customers ask you to. But it is your job to take a step back and really hear what your customers are saying. What is the through-line in all of the feedback? Identify it and move. Speed is critical in today's marketplace, especially SaaS (software as a service). If you aren't working to incrementally improve your product, someone else will fill the gap.

Speed to market and constant iteration are necessary in today's market. Being able to make decisions quickly and bring them to life is more important than having a perfect plan in place. All it takes is the next right step, then the next right step after that to keep you moving forward and aligned with your customers' needs.

Diversity Makes Us Better

Pavilion is diverse, and our team needs to be diverse to ensure we appreciate all perspectives. Diversity strengthens us. Diversity forces us to appreciate different perspectives, to empathize; it forces open our minds like a crowbar opening a dusty vault. To be better, to be our best, we need to value everyone and mean it.

"Value everyone and mean it" is the key phrase here. As I said, it's easy to slap up some surface-level values that you never do anything about. It's easy to talk and say something performative you know will make you or your company appear better in the public eye.

But values need to be actionable. For us, Diversity Makes Us Better is a call to look for a range of voices and experiences and actively bring them into our business.

From a panel discussion to our executive team, we strive to champion a diverse set of voices in everything that we do. I'm proud to say that as of March 1, 2022, 54% of the Pavilion HQ team identifies as female and 36% self-reported as Black, Indigenous, or Person of Color (BIPOC). That includes 60% female leadership on the executive team.

Within our membership, we have created private spaces for Women of Pavilion, Pavilion of Color, and LGTBQ+ of Pavilion to provide a safe place where they can talk about challenges they face and be supported. Why does this matter? Because we believe that in order to achieve and unlock your professional potential, you should be able to tap into your full self without fear of judgment. We believe that by having an HQ team that reflects the diversity of our membership, we will be better able to understand them and to serve them.

So if your company says it values diversity, think about the tangible ways you are working to make sure diverse voices are heard and respected in your space.

We Deliver Results

The great thing about how we've structured our values is that there is room to grow. Our mission and North Star (Members First) always stay true, but how can we adapt over time and make room for more.

Originally, this value was "Always Better." We wanted to be a company that never finished evolving, changing, and trying to improve. We valued feedback as a way to keep learning and unlock change and innovation. All of that is still true, but in practice we found that "Always Better" was not specific enough to serve as a guide for decision making.

In the spirit of "Always Better," we evolved to incorporate a new value—we deliver results.

Results matter. We are focused on achieving our goals. That includes a sense of personal responsibility for our performance and outcomes. If we're reporting on a number, we take responsibility for that number. If we set a goal, we commit to reaching that goal. We proactively communicate along the way. We don't hide. We understand that we can't deliver on our promise to our Members and to each other if goals don't matter, if results don't matter, and we aren't doing everything we can to help the company grow. We want to look to our left and to our right, even if virtually, and trust that everyone on the Pavilion team is committed to holding up their end of the bargain. Results matter.

"We Deliver Results" speaks to why we need to always be improving. We are improving for a reason, and that reason is to deliver specific results for our Members and for our business. Our Members have goals, and we help achieve them. Our business has goals, and we will be numbers-beaters. By baking results into the values of our organization we instill in all of our employees—and in our Members—a sense of ownership. We are in charge of our own destinies and our own projects. If we say we will do something, we do it.

Think about the values at your organization. Do you explicitly say that you value outcomes? If not, what message does that send to your team and your customers?

From the beginning, we used the Objectives and Key Results (OKR) framework to build annual and quarterly goals for the organization as a whole. But in 2022, we incorporated OKRs at the department and individual levels, too. Individual OKRs roll up into department OKRs, and department OKRs roll up into the company-wide OKRs.

By aligning individual goals with your department and then the overarching organizational goals, you ensure that everyone will be rowing in the same direction. We see within our membership endless debate around aligning sales and marketing, marketing and customer success, customer success and sales. It goes on and on. We found that by incorporating a value based on results and building a framework where all individuals understand how their actions impact the larger organization, alignment has come naturally.

We Choose to Come from Kindness

Kindness begets more kindness. Every action we take comes from a place of empathy and compassion. We treat our teammates and our Members with the compassion and empathy they deserve as human beings. We try to pass along the legacy of compassion, empathy, and understanding in every interaction, even when delivering bad news or constructive criticism. We are honest and direct, but we don't use that as an excuse to be an asshole. We don't blow up a meeting with temper tantrums. We don't act like children. The world is better when people are kind. We choose to come from kindness.

The wording of this value came from Pavilion's VP of partnerships and alliances, and I love how it was written. We *choose* to come from kindness. We make an active choice every day to approach each interaction with empathy and understanding. Even if it is a tough conversation. Especially if it is a tough conversation.

Being kind doesn't mean you are a pushover. Or that you sugar-coat bad news to save people's feelings. Or that you never scowl or are in a bad mood. My team will tell you that my mood fluctuates, and I have a hard time hiding it.

Choosing to come from kindness means that you understand and respect that everyone has a lot going on in their lives. That you first come from a supportive place looking to help others improve or achieve their goals.

The world is insistent that you need to toughen up, to have a thick skin. In business, we've been told to relentlessly pursue our goals, and you need to be a bit ruthless to truly make it to the top.

But you know that I believe there is a larger table with room for everyone. Some might take advantage of your kindness. But many, many more won't. And in the end, what you will remember are the people you've helped and the difference you made.

Choosing to come from kindness means that you don't need to keep score of everyone who has wronged you. You don't need to constantly remind people you could fire them. You don't need to put people down.

Choosing to come from kindness means knowing that every good deed you put out in the world comes back to you tenfold. The title of this book says it all. Choosing to come from kindness is how nice folks finish first.

WHAT'S NEXT

As we have scaled, these values have guided our course. That's what corporate values should do. When faced with a difficult choice, you will have a clear framework of how you should make decisions. Strong corporate values won't solve every problem your business will face, but they will solve many problems.

If you take the time to develop what you stand for through the exercise included in Chapter 3, you can deploy a similar framework that I used with Revenue Collective and Pavilion. Start with what you stand for, distill your top values into clear, specific guidelines for your team, and always follow your North Star. Then, you will always know the next right step.

CHAPTER 5 TACTICS: WHAT ARE YOUR VALUES?

I had never understood the true power of values until I spent time with Brian Litvack, whose company LeagueApps lived and died by their values. They had created an acronym, SPORTSDOG, which was a reference to their sports background and put a heavy emphasis on teamwork and collaboration.

I remember conversations with Brian where he remarked that running the company was made a lot easier by the presence of these values. Every decision, conflict, or controversy could reference the values, and it made it so much easier to drive autonomous decision making.

Again, remembering that metaphor of navigating through a forest, if you have the plan and you have the values, you should be able to get where you want to go.

To that end, take 30 minutes to write down your belief system and begin to think about how to make those words resonant and meaningful for you. Don't just write down "Innovation" but think about the ideas and the slogans you find yourself repeating often. Then unpack them to understand what they really mean to you.

This is the exercise that gave rise to "Listen closely, act quickly" and "X+Y."

CHAPTER 6

Listen Closely, Act Quickly

This chapter is about things you need to understand to build a business. We go a little deep on the order of operations, the power of marketing, and how to think about growing a company. This book, after all, is a combination of principles you employ as a professional to access your objectives and succeed, and it's also about the steps I took embodying other principles in business design.

As we'll see, the core of both being a great professional and building a company are often the same. And it begins with listening closely.

With a two-person HQ team, Revenue Collective continued to grow in 2019, using email as the primary communication tool. People would email questions and get answers with everyone on the chain.

This was, and still is, a pretty standard format for a community, and many communities employ different versions of this simple idea.

But as membership steadily grew around the world, we pivoted from email to Slack—and saw our growth explode. Nowadays, Slack is a very common community management tool, but back in 2019, it was a relatively new interface.

Where did this idea come from? Well, from our Members, of course. One of our longtime Members, and a good friend of mine, was a huge foodie and had worked with some of the best restaurant minds out there. He also happened to be a forward-thinking technology enthusiast (his current role combines these two loves). He kept calling me and basically yelled at me to move Revenue Collective conversations to Slack.

In 2019, we finally had critical mass. We took that leap and it paid off.

LISTENING IS THE KEY

Today, 30% of our membership engages in Slack every week. In 2021, we had more than a million messages sent across our Slack workspaces. We have hundreds of channels, predominantly built from Member suggestions with Members who step up to moderate and guide conversations.

Some of our most popular Slack channels have taken on a life of their own, spurring regular, virtual meetups of thousands of Members, and even Pavilion University courses.

All of this evolved organically with Member feedback guiding the way. The most interesting part to me is that this was not built with proprietary technology. We built this community with solutions that were already available to us and that we have tweaked and adapted as we have grown.

As we talked about in Chapter 5, so many people over-complicate their strategy. They think they need to have the perfect solution in place before they launch. But what you really need to do is listen to your customers and meet their needs with the resources you have.

In today's world, especially in B2B software, speed is more important than perfect. People need a solution fast, and are willing to join you as you iterate improvements if the majority of their needs are met.

Slack enabled us to grow and foster conversations with Members across the world, especially during lockdowns and pandemic travel restrictions.

Three years later, we are getting more feedback about how noisy Slack has become, and our Members long for more intimate conversations and closer connections after so many years of remote and virtual meetings.

And that's okay. It's okay to move on from or make adjustments to something that once served you so well—if that's what your customers want.

That's why we are engineering a Pavilion-created Member portal, taking all of the disparate platforms on which we operate and streamlining the experience into a central Pavilion hub. As our membership grows and as the world changes, the needs of Members change. And we are open to their feedback and adapting with them.

This is to say, your customers should be the ones driving your direction. If you listen to what your customers truly need, you'll be able to act on it quickly and gain their long-term trust.

THE RIGHT WAY TO SCALE

From my own LinkedIn page to Pavilion University lectures to mega industry conferences, I have spoken about the right way to scale many, many times. Yet, I still see businesses today get it wrong.

I start any speaking engagement on this topic with a simple question: What makes a great company?

Is it raising a lot of money? Culture built around a set of shared values? Naps?

I believe that great culture is actually the exhaust of a high-performing organization. If you're winning and succeeding, then that is the context for having a great culture.

And high-performing organizations are the ones that attract investment dollars.

And while Pavilion is a firmly pro-nap, values-based organization, the thing that great companies actually do is profitably and repeatedly regenerate returns on invested capital.

That is what scaling a business really means—profitable repeatability. And you can get there if you take the right steps, listening closely to your customers every step of the way and acting with urgency.

The Market as a Proxy for the Universe

Your customers are the market. And the market represents the universe.

Stick with me here.

Energy flows throughout the universe and for you to be an effective conduit of that energy, you must first learn to be still. This is the mechanism for achieving your wildest dreams. There's a reason that meditation, journaling, and similar practices are exalted by your favorite business leaders. When you are able to tap into the natural flow of the universe, that is when you experience personal growth.

Or if you are less spiritually inclined, think about when you get your best ideas. Is it in the shower? Or on a walk? When you're about to fall asleep? The times where your mind is still and isn't racing through your to-do list are when you are most receptive to what is happening around you. You can receive information, react to what is presented to you, and choose what to do about it more easily.

In the same regard, you must listen closely to what your customers are saying in order to unlock business growth. Alignment and the conduction of energy is in many ways what a company is intended to do. The very phrase "product-market fit" alludes to that concept. The market, your customers, fits the product, which is the thing you are building.

How do you get them to fit? Is it a self-centered and egotistical leap into the great unknown powered only by your creativity and genius? If that were the case, then where did your genius arise from in the first place? What does genius even mean?

Your genius lies in your ability to listen to forces greater than yourself and align yourself with those forces. Genius lies in actively swimming with the current, not against it.

So when the market tells you what it's looking for, listen. Then act quickly to deliver that product.

Building a Customer-Centric Product

I believe the product is the thing that determines how fast you should grow, whether you should grow, and whether you're in a position to grow.

Your product needs to address the concerns you've heard from your customers. It needs to solve their problems. So many companies and organizations call themselves customer-first but fail to employ the simplest ideas to ensure they are building the products and services their customers want.

Too many people have read the Steve Jobs's biography and are convinced they know better than their customers. Of course, Apple builds consumer products, not business-to-business software. And of course we're not all Steve Jobs. Rather than taking one anomaly and trying to apply it to a completely different market, just step back and listen. Your customers will tell you what they want.

It again comes back to loving your customers. I've worked at places where they did create a product that addressed a large market problem. But the customers weren't their North Star. Their technology was. This caused friction between the company and customers, resulting in slower growth and less predictable revenue. Customers still need to be at the center of what you do in order to reach your fullest potential as a business. A customer-centric product is a sure-fire way to generate demand.

Again, the idea here is straightforward. Not easy. But simple.

The essential quality in building a customer-centric business is empathy. Putting yourself in the shoes of your customer and really trying to understand and appreciate where they are coming from. That's why so many great companies are started by people that experienced that particular problem. Because the founders had empathy.

The quality most related to empathy is the ability to listen.

Practice it. Work on it. Listening comes from the ability to be still. Your movements create noise. Your speech creates noise. Your desire to be noticed and important and to show people how smart you are creates noise.

So how can you walk softly, to bastardize Teddy Roosevelt, so that you can hear the universe when it wants to speak to you. That's the trick. Embrace the stillness. Embrace other people's perspectives. Truly try to understand their feedback so that you can turn it around in your head and really process it.

Generating Demand

This is the stage where most companies get out of order. So many organizations look at their large market and amazing product designed with customer input and start hiring sales reps.

But salespeople don't generate demand.

It seems counterintuitive because I came up through the sales world. But I am a salesperson who believes sales is the least important discipline when scaling. What salespeople are great at is turning demand into revenue. And in order for your sales team to close deals, they need leads.

So who generates demand? Marketing. The least expensive way to bring in customers is to have a great product that people love, that they tell their friends about. A great marketing organization understands how to amplify that message to tell more and more people at large, repeating that message out to a bigger and bigger audience.

Only after word spreads across the market, piquing interest, does a prospect enter a structured buying conversation with your sales team.

The most reliable way to scale and predictably generate revenue is to start with a really, really big market. Then, comes a great, customer-centric product. Next, you need to be able to tell your market about the product in a structured and effective way. And only then can you turn that demand into revenue.

The Power of Marketing

Marketing is the act of delivering a specific message to a specific group of people, at a specific time, in order to compel them to make a decision. And yet, it's also much bigger than that. It's your brand. It's how people feel about your company or product. What emotions come up for them.

Too many people misunderstand marketing or try to reduce it down to some easily definable essence. "Marketing is lead generation." No. Not really. It's bigger than that. Or it's longer term than that at least.

Because it's not just about getting new people interested in your product today. It's about making them happy and giving them messages through your brand that make them want to be interested today, tomorrow, and months and years into the future.

Again tying it back to some organic concept of the universe (here he goes again with the universe), marketing is about harnessing the atomic power of your customers' love and appreciation for your product to create a megaphone that broadcasts that love outwards. A clear powerfully broadcast message with a specific intended audience, with a point of view, can reach far and wide and bring people to your door.

And from there, your sales team kicks into gear to help those people become customers and engage properly with your product.

Too many people make the mistake of under-investing in marketing, thinking it's just brochures, or it's just one-pagers, or it's just the website.

It's so much more than that. So take the time to treat it with the care, love, and respect it deserves.

Revenue Is a Team Sport

The essence of all of this is that making money is not just one person or team's department. Making money is the combination of all of the pieces coming together. And in that sense it's a much longer-term project than we sometimes assume. It's not about driving something someone doesn't need down their throat. It's about building something people love, something that is not apart from them but, in some way, comes from them both directly and indirectly.

All of the pieces fit into place when you have a great product that people love, people want to tell other people about how much they love it, and then you harness and amplify that enthusiasm to tell the world. That's how it works.

Sales is a piece of all of that but not the essence. The essence is the entire movement, in combination and orchestration.

Put another way, salespeople don't generate demand. They turn demand into money. But demand is the essence. In today's world, with the ubiquity of information and with everything on a review site, salespeople can't just tell a customer how the world is. The customer already knows how the world is. Salespeople can help answer questions, can see if there's a fit with that person's needs, and if so convert them into being a customer.

PHASES OF GROWTH

Now that you know the right way to scale, how do you decide when it's time to make a move? Again, I say, listen to your customers.

In the early, early days of a business—around five customers—that is the time to focus on product-market fit. Gather input from your customers and only move forward if you can retain 90% of those customers with 100% revenue retention and have a Net Promoter Score (NPS) greater than 30.

We use NPS at Pavilion, and while there are other metrics you can track and arguments against it, I think it is the easiest way to measure if your product is meeting the needs of your customers. NPS asks customers to rate how likely they are to recommend your product or service on a scale of 1 to 10. People who rate you 1 through 6 are considered detractors, those who rate you 7 or 8 are neutral and not factored into the NPS equation, and only 9s and 10s are considered promoters.

Where some of the debate comes in, is that some founders will lie when they're raising their decks and say that NPS is an average rating of customer satisfaction. It is not an average rating. It is the percent of people who are promoters less the percent of people who are detractors. It is not the average score that you get on a customer satisfaction survey.

So if you are looking at a 30 NPS score, it might mean that 50% of people are promoters and 20% are detractors.

If you hit these metrics in the product-market fit phase, then that is a signal that you are ready to move to the next stage of business growth—go-to-market fit.

I use these metrics and reference them because they are fairly standard assessments of customer health. Remember when we talked about the power of the market? These numbers are reflections of the market because they are reflections of your customers. And these benchmarks are effectively industry standards for signals that would indicate an opportunity to invest and grow.

The essence of them is straightforward—these are numbers that are telling you that people like your product or service. If your customers stick around in large numbers, you have a good thing going. If they leave or are generally dissatisfied, you have a problem. The basics of my philosophy are that if you are seeing increases in people leaving, you should generally consider pausing before adding investments in growth. Because all you'll be doing is growing into customers that will give your product a shot and then decide to leave. And if you do that, you don't have a sustainable business. And that's what we're trying to build.

We've gone through a lot of ups and downs at Pavilion, and the core of our focus and our business has always been Net Promoter Score. We want people to love our product. We want them to have amazing experiences, and we want them to be raving fans of what we do.

Importantly, the other thing to note and to emphasize is that we're not looking generally at a point in time but trying always to understand the trend. One data point at what point in time is somewhat useful. Multiple data points measured consistently are powerful because you can begin to understand which way your customers are moving and spot certain inflection points or trends.

We noticed a dip in Net Promoter Score at Pavilion back at the end of 2020. We'd grown tremendously during COVID and had been pushing big membership growth through a variety of different campaigns. We had become too enamored of growth for its own sake, and our customers started noticing the difference in our tone and in our emphasis. So our NPS began to fall. In a vacuum, the numbers were still pretty good. But it was the trend that was important.

And we made adjustments. So make sure as you evaluate these metrics that you are not just looking at a point in time but specifically looking at the trend line.

Once you see positive indications over time in your retention and your NPS, you are ready to move to more active attempts to scale.

This is the phase where you will bring on someone to manage marketing, craft your messaging, and start generating demand. You should then hire your first sales reps to close on that demand and customer success managers to retain your current customers, keep them happy, and potentially upsell or expand their contracts.

As you grow to 20 customers, you should still be able to retain 90% of customers and 100% of revenue with a NPS score greater than 30. The next metric you'll want to measure is a payback period of less than 12 months or less than one sales cycle. We'll go through how to measure this below, but go-to-market fit is a crucial step in determining whether the cost of acquiring a customer is worth it.

Only then can you move onto the final phase, which I call scalable growth. My advice here is to hire based on capacity relative to demand generation, and always be sure you are maintaining the baseline metrics from the previous stages.

THE IMPORTANCE OF UNIT ECONOMICS

Unit economics tell the core story of your business and whether it is designed in a way that ultimately works. They distill all of the churn, all of the big macro trends into an evaluation of dollars per customer.

So what does the phrase "unit economics" mean anyhow? Here's what it means at its core. It means understanding the basic sales and marketing motion and understanding the relationship between how much money a typical customer pays you, how much you paid to acquire them, and how quickly.

How much are you spending to get this customer? How much do they pay us back and over what time period? That's what unit economics will tell you. A simple premise, but so rich in terms of operating a business successfully.

Now, you might be thinking, I'm a salesperson who doesn't do spreadsheets. Sales is about relationships, and the most important thing is to form a relationship with your customers, right?

But if you want to be in an executive role, you need to realize that you can't just focus on one aspect of the business. You also need to know spreadsheets because they, too, tell a story of the business. It's another way to listen closely, but with the data to back up your actions.

What Goes into Unit Economics: Customer Acquisition Cost

We can get into the math of it but again as I mentioned earlier, the basics of the math are that you take all of the costs associated with acquiring a customer and add them up. Those costs include the salaries of all your salespeople and their benefits, the salaries of most of the people that work on marketing for you, even the salaries of some of your support folks that spend most of their time working with existing customers but occasionally hop on a call with a prospect to tell them what it's really like being a customer.

You also add in all the money you're spending on marketing programs—things like the plane trip you took to Indianapolis to meet with a big potential customer, the steak dinner you wined and dined them with, the big conference you sponsored where you hosted a booth and scanned a bunch of name tags, and, of course, any money you're spending advertising on places like LinkedIn, Google, Instagram, TikTok, and anywhere else.

This is what we call Customer Acquisition Cost, or CAC. Don't be a child and make some funny joke about the acronym (unless that joke is so absurdly funny *South Park*–style that despite all the people it rightfully offends for its childish infantilism, it still elicits a chuckle).

When you are thinking about CAC, the point is that you don't want to be too optimistic. You want to be conservative. You want to add in all the possible things you're doing to get people interested in your product. All the people you're hiring. All the money you're spending.

Importantly, this is only money you are spending to "acquire" the customer, not to serve them. This isn't the R&D you're doing to build a new product, and it's not the staff you're paying to make sure once your customers are sold, they're happy. But this is everything else.

Your temptation when building your analysis will be to take some things out. Maybe you just hired a salesperson and you don't feel it's fair to include them in the calculation. They just started after all, and they're still in their ramp period. My advice is to avoid that temptation and to try and include every possible cost you can to be as realistic as possible.

We're not trying to spin when we think about how much it takes to get someone to try our wonderful beautiful product. We're trying to understand the actual tangible cost.

To the point of values espoused in this weighty tome we call a book (not really that weighty, I'm sure this is solidly in the quite light category, maybe should've been an essay-length book), doing things the right way takes time. *Kind Folks Finish First* isn't about shortcuts, and it isn't about schemes. These aren't schemes. All the things we're talking about (again with the parentheticals but obviously nobody is talking, you're reading and I'm writing) take a certain amount of time. The values in this book, the beliefs I'm articulating, are not about grabbing everything you can as quickly as you can, and they're not about lying to yourself. They're about trusting that if you work earnestly and pains-takingly in service of other people (in this case your customers) that you'll succeed.

So put everything you can think of into your Customer Acquisition Cost. That's the first key element.

What Goes into Unit Economics: Gross Margin

The next thing we're going to do once we have CAC is to understand our Gross Margin. The essential way of thinking about Gross Margin is the marginal cost of delivering one more unit of the product.

In the old days, it was pretty easy to calculate. If you made widgets, you'd calculate the cost of making the widget and producing it, including the cost of the materials, and you'd subtract that from your revenue, and that would be your gross margin.

Software and services are a bit more theoretical. Because, again, it's about "How much does it cost you to deliver the product itself?" If you're being extremely sunny, you'll just take out your web hosting costs under the assumption that "Hey this is software, the beauty of it is that one more unit of the product is just the money I'm paying

Amazon Web Services to power the website and the app, and it's infinitesimal."

Maybe. But probably not.

Because if you need any humans to support the delivery of the product, you need to include them in the calculation. These days we call those people Customer Success. It's a function that makes sense and has existed for ages but was really formally popularized by Nick Mehta and Anthony Kennada when they built the software company Gainsight.

And these days almost everyone realizes that to make people actually use something, it takes humans teaching them and coaching them through the best practices, checking on them regularly to see how things are going, and ensuring that the customers are mapping and aligning their specific business goals with the actual uses of the product you've built.

All of that is part of the marginal cost of delivering the service, and all of it should be put into Gross Margin. As I mentioned above, if some portion of the time of your Customer Success Team is allocated to talking to prospects with the Sales Team then put that percentage into CAC, but all of the salaries and investments you make in Customer Success should go in either CAC or Gross Margin.

At Pavilion, our Gross Margin has another wrinkle because from the very beginning we've paid our Chapter Heads, the community managers that helped us build the global network. The very first folks like Tom Glason in London and Rich Gardner in Boston made as much as 90% of the total dues at one point. These days we've thankfully renegotiated those deals, and our community managers make a flat monthly retainer based on total number of Members in their chapter.

So when we calculate Gross Margin we put in 25% of the marketing team's time and money (the other 75% goes into CAC), 100% of the Member Success Team (that's what we call Customer Success), and we even allocate some of my salary as the CEO both to CAC and Gross Margin. We also add in the software we use to support our Members (like Slack or Airtable or any one of the myriad services we use), and, of course, we take out the Chapter Head payments. These days those payments come out to anywhere between $150,000 to $200,000.

Add it all up and that's effectively our Cost of Goods Sold. Subtract that from our monthly membership dues, and the result is our Gross Margin. Even though some might call us a services business, our Gross Margin is still pretty good hovering around the 70% range. Great software businesses have 80% gross margins, and that's why they're so fantastic. Ours is still pretty good (cue the Larry David impression).

What Goes into Unit Economics: Churn

Not every business is a subscription business, but every business wants their customers to stick around and buy more stuff or to come back quickly once they buy the first thing.

Churn is most common when looking at subscription businesses but it's a concept that can be applied anywhere. And it's not rocket science. It's simply the percent of your customers and the money they spend that walks out the door in any given time period.

For subscription businesses, it's the lagging indicator that NPS might first alert you to. And it's fundamental.

Since it's really describing whether people like the thing you've built or not.

I've been in some hilarious investor meetings where the venture capital investor speaks of churn as sort of an abstract variable. "If you just fix churn by 10%, you'll easily hit the number," which is very funny if you think about it since what you're saying is "If you just make people like your thing 10% more, you'll hit the number." Well, the entire business, the whole point of everything, is to make people like your thing; so yeah, thank you for the input, we are working on it!

For most businesses that sell to consumers like Netflix, a great number is 2% monthly churn which means 2% of your customers walk out the door every month.

If you can't solve churn then, of course, you have to add more customers to make up the difference.

And this is also why market size is so important because you need enough people that love what you do and that find it regularly valuable that they don't leave and they do stick around.

When we analyze churn, we want to look at it by groups of customers or cohorts. For companies that sell to other companies (B2B), you might have a lever you can pull that makes things a lot better, which is expansion revenue.

This means that you might sell a customer a set of goods or services in January, but over the course of the year they tend to buy more stuff from you. Maybe they add more users. Maybe they increase their usage.

But if, on average, your customers as a group tend to spend more collectively at the end of the time period, you are doing really well. We call that number Net Revenue Retention and it means what percent of the total sale do you tend to keep after a typical time period, say a year.

Great businesses keep upwards of 125% of their original spend. Companies like Snowflake Computing have 140% NRR or more at time.

It's tough to get there but if you do, you have something magical.

But the bottom line is pretty straightforward. Churn is the measurement of whether people actually stick around. If people stick around, you've got something. If they leave, something is broken.

More than anything else, churn is the number in your financial statements that tells you whether the thing you've built is working or not.

The Four Core Pieces of Unit Economics

So the four core pieces of unit economics are how much you have to pay to acquire a customer (CAC), how much they pay you in return (this is Revenue; I didn't do a section on this since hopefully it's obvious; it's that you know the money your customers pay you for the thing), Gross Margin, and churn with the number of customers you acquire being the final key variable and telling you your average sale price as well.

Think of it this way:

Businesses are money machines. They are designed to take in some amount of money to produce something, run it through the machine, and then spit out more money at the bottom, almost like the game Plinko on the *Price Is Right*.

The way they do this is they use money that's left over from servicing their customers or they use investor capital.

As a business is growing, you might be making tons of investments that pay returns over a long period of time. You might be hiring lots of engineers to write code, you might be doing a ton of R&D on potential new products, you might be building new retail locations that have amazing experiences inside them (like my wife's store The Seven in the West Village, which if you haven't visited you absolutely must, it's amazing).

But all that money is not the core unit economics. Those are investments.

So when you're trying to understand if a business is any good, what you need to understand is that if you strip away all the investments and all the money you might be taking out of the business, if you just look at the core mechanics, is it a good business?

You spend money to acquire customers, they pay you your fees, you then spend money to service those customers, and what's left over from all of that can either be taken out of the business (look at the nice new motorcycle you just bought yourself) or reinvested back into the business to keep it growing and to build new stuff.

But at the core, if you're spending too much to acquire a customer and they're not paying you back enough, or it's costing too much or they leave too soon, then you might have a bad business.

And, again, because repetition is important, this is very much related to the core values that we're talking about. This is about generosity and playing for the long term. Because at the core, the way to build a great product is to make it not about you. It's about your customers. It's about listening to them. It's about tinkering on the margins to make them happier. It's not about your brilliance. Building a great product and correspondingly a great company is about service. Being in service to your customers.

One Last Metric: Lifetime Value

If you know your CAC (again, resist the urge to make a silly joke), your Gross Margin, and your churn, you can calculate your unit economics, and you can start to understand if you've got a good business or not.

One of the most important ratios you might calculate is Lifetime Value. Lifetime Value is simple—it's the average Gross Margin per customer divided by churn. What it means is this: What's the total value of the money your customers contribute to your business over the lifetime of their relationship with you.

You compare Lifetime Value to your Customer Acquisition Cost to understand what I reference above— how much do you spend to acquire a customer, and is it worth it depending on how much they pay you back in total over the life of their relationship?

David Skok, famous investor and entrepreneur and founding partner at Matrix Partners, says the ideal ratio is 3:1. That means that on average your customers pay you 3 times more than it costs to acquire them. I prefer 5:1 mostly because even if I'm being conservative I still think I tend to be too rosy in my assumptions and want to try and bake in as much cushion as possible.

Again, this is important stuff. Why? Because it's fundamental. It's "Do people like my thing enough to stick around and pay me more and make up for how hard it is to convince them to try it out in the first place?"

Put another way, they have to stick around. They have to come back. And they have to think it's worth enough to run the business.

Sometimes folks ask me, "What if my lifetime value is low because the most I can charge for my product doesn't cover the cost of acquiring the customer?" And my response is unfortunately a bit smart assy. Because if that's your situation, then you don't have a good product, and you're in the wrong market.

The fundamental group that gets to decide how much your product is worth is your customer, which is another way of saying the market, which is another way of saying it's not about you and your time and how hard anything is for you. This isn't about you. It's about them. Period.

The Final Ratio (for Now and in This Book, There Are Obviously Lots of Ratios): Payback Period

Lifetime Value is important, but the most important metric in my opinion when it comes to this stuff is Payback Period. Payback Period just means: "How long till I recoup my costs so I can put the money back into the business?"

Again, think of boiling these ideas down to their essence. If you spend a ton of money to get someone to try your product and they pay you only a little bit of money, even if they stick around, it's going to take you a long-ass time to funnel the proceeds back into the business to get more customers.

The very best businesses have short payback periods, which is a way of saying your customers pay you a lot and your cost of servicing them is low (high Gross Margin) so that you can quickly take the profits from acquiring them and servicing them and reinvest those profits back into the business to get even more customers or to build new products or to pay yourself a nice fat dividend.

We calculate a cash-based payback period at Pavilion (vs. calculating reported revenue, which is not always the same as cash) and historically have been paid back on our investments in under one time period. On an annual basis, that means we get paid back under 12 months which is fantastic.

Just like a bad Lifetime Value (LTV) to CAC ratio, if it takes a long time to get paid back on your acquisition efforts, something is broken in your business. In any given time period, the Payback Period might move around. For example, we did a bunch of in-person conferences in 2022 that cost a lot of money but didn't pay us back in the form of new Members very quickly. So in the short term, our Payback Period suffered. But generally speaking, our Payback Period has been around 10 months at scale.

Investors will tell you that 18, maybe even 24 months, is an acceptable Payback Period. But think about what that means. That means that when you spend a dollar, you don't see the full benefits of that dollar for over a year and a half. *Maron*. That's a heckuva long time. So much in the world can change in a year and a half. And more importantly, if you want to keep growing, you're going to need another source of cash than revenue. You're going to need investment.

So I get that lots of people out there think that 18 months is fine, but I think when people really love your thing and when you've designed a simple beautiful machine that's built around the needs and wants of your customers, they'll tell you more emphatically and sooner than in a year and a half. That's just me though. You do you.

Here are my four tips for evaluating unit economics:

1. **Match your evaluation period to your sales cycle**
   If your sales cycle is 18 months, you'll want to compare how much you spent over 18 months and how much you got back over 18 months. Of course, we'd love to get the money back more quickly, but it's only fair to evaluate the whole thing based on your average sales cycle. Another good reason to push for quick sales cycles.

2. **Fully load all sales and marketing costs, including headcount**
   As I wrote above, you'll be tempted to take a bunch of money you spend that feels iffy and keep it out to make the numbers look better. But put everything in there, even the new people that don't know what they're doing. You want your CAC and Gross Margin calculations to be as thorough and comprehensive as possible.

3. **Add in any marketing spend and variable acquisition costs**
   In my opinion, you should add in any marketing spend and variable acquisition cost. That includes paid acquisition, the conference that you went to, the client dinner, even the plane tickets that were needed to take the customers to dinner. You should include as many of the costs as you can to get a more accurate picture. If you start removing costs from the equation, that's when you start getting into funny stuff territory.

4. **No funny stuff**

> To me, funny stuff would include things like only looking at the customer acquisition cost (CAC) for fully ramped account executives, when you have several unramped AEs on your payroll. That is still a cost you need to factor in.

You can debate what goes into CAC and what goes into gross margin. Should you include hosting cost in gross margin? Should you include the CEO salary in gross margin? I certainly know CFOs and CEOs who are in the fundraising process who would exclude those costs to try to lower the CAC.

I think you should factor it all into CAC. That is money you're spending, and you want to look at it honestly. Believe me, the longer you lie to yourself the harder it will be to unwind that lie later. It is only when you are honest about the truths uncovered by unit economics that you can go about fixing them.

RULES OF THUMB

Once you have all of your numbers loaded in, divide relevant time period bookings by CAC to understand your payback period.

If the payback period is less than 9 months, that is an incredible business. Invest in that business, or find investors if that is your business, immediately. Nine to 12 months is still good, but things start to get dicier in the 12–16 month range. Up to 24 months, the business is not looking good, and anything over 24 months means something is fundamentally broken in the business.

COMMON MISTAKES TO AVOID

There are three mistakes I see most often when it comes to unit economics:

1. Assuming your customer acquisition cost will get better over time

2. Assuming your early habit of underpaying is sustainable long term

3. Assuming no one will notice the funny stuff

There could be an argument for a U-shaped curve where CAC gets better with true market penetration, when everyone knows your product. But, generally speaking, your CAC is going to get worse as your company grows. That's because you're reaching out to people who are further and further afield from the people who were originally interested in buying your product. You need to expand your reach and spend more time educating and nurturing. That costs money.

When you underpay your early hires, it might seem like you have this amazing ratio between lifetime value (LTV) and CAC. But, if you want to attract and retain the kind of talent who will make you profitable, you'll need to pay market rate. Underpaying your employees is not sustainable, and being a bad place to work is the kind of reputation that will get back to your customers. Then you will become an organization that's bad to do business with.

And as I mentioned earlier, funny stuff like manipulating the numbers is a costly error. The earliest investors in your business might be easier to fool as they are just as enthusiastic about your product as you are, but in later fundraising stages people will do real due diligence. Funny stuff will not fly.

Now, I'm not telling you all of this because I am an all-knowing sales being. I'm telling you this because I have learned these lessons the hard way. I hadn't listened to my customers. I hadn't acted in their best interests. I got fired.

These are lessons I am sharing with you from personal experience, and I know I would have benefited from somebody helping me understand how to actually evaluate a business.

THE WRONG WAY TO SCALE

When I was working at Axial between 2010 and 2015 (the place where I tried to get the CEO fired), we didn't have product-market fit, but we had raised a lot of money.

So, I hired more and more people—sales development reps, account executives, customer success managers. The executive team felt so much pressure to be a company that we weren't, and we were told by investors that we needed to grow our annual recurring revenue (ARR).

We started running promotions. New customers signed on, paying for 10 months and getting 2 months free. The problem with that is ARR dashboards are annualized. That per month payment was multiplied across 12 months, making it seem like more money was coming in each year than there actually was.

When our next round of funding came up, I put together the term sheet outlining our financials and celebrated with the team.

Thinking the deal was in the bag, I left on my honeymoon with Camille and expected to return to news of more investments. Instead, the deal fell through.

I received a call no one wants to get, especially on their honeymoon. I screwed up.

I had to leave my honeymoon early to come back home and clean up the mess. It was one of the most humiliating and terrible moments of my life, albeit a formative and powerful one.

Trying not to make the same mistakes at Livestream, where I landed after Axial, I wanted to understand our customers better. When upselling current customers wasn't working, I found that the same people were coming back a few times a year when they needed our service and then canceling their subscription.

Thinking I had found our mistake, I hired a demand-generation manager to bring in more leads. Remember, a great marketing organization understands how to amplify a message. And the best messaging comes from your customers and how they talk about your product.

Again I jumped too far ahead. We didn't have a compelling message or a base of content addressing the pain points we heard from our customers. The demand-gen person had no message to amplify.

We pitched the board, but didn't grow as we promised we would. Another lesson in scaling the wrong way.

Then at The Muse, I lowered the target, trying not to mess this up again. But too high of a target wasn't the issue at Axial and Livestream. It was a misunderstanding of the order of operations.

By the time I went full time with Revenue Collective, I got it. I started with a large market, and built something that people were asking me for. We grew organically by word of mouth, then I brought on a great marketer to harness that customer sentiment and to form messaging that would accelerate existing demand. And by the end of 2020, we hired enrollment managers to handle that inbound demand and turn them into paying Members. An outbound sales motion didn't exist at Pavilion until 2021, five years after we'd started.

The right way to scale is to follow the correct order of operations, deeply understand your unit economics, and underpin everything you do with a love and appreciation for your customers. This is what will enable you to act quickly and delight your customers.

I finally got scaling right, but there was something looming on the horizon that would test our values and force us to back up all of our principles with action. The onset of the COVID-19 pandemic forever changed our lives and the nature of Revenue Collective.

CHAPTER 6 TACTICS

Core SaaS Metric Definitions

CAC = Customer Acquisition Cost

The cost related to acquiring a new customer calculated by totaling all of the money you spend in the acquisition, including sales and marketing head count and other costs.

LTV = Lifetime Value

A prediction of the net profit attributed to an ongoing relationship between customer and product calculated by multiplying the average purchase value by the average number of purchases.

LTV:CAC Ratio

How much money you'll make per customer over how much it cost to acquire them.

Payback Period

The time to recover your CAC on average per customer.

Churn

The number of or monetary value of customers lost per time period.

NPS = Net Promoter Score

Measures customer experience of your brand by calculating the percent of customers who are promoters less the percent of customers who are detractors.

CHAPTER 7

Every Crisis Is an Opportunity

We're jumping ahead in the timeline of my revelations a bit, but I think this is the right opportunity to talk about operating on kind principles during a crisis—something there's no shortage of these days.

By early 2020, I was pouring all of my time and energy into Revenue Collective. And we surged. Dedicated chapters sprung up in London, Boston, Toronto. All focused on bringing people together, bonding over shared experiences, and offering support to those who needed it. This vision was taking hold.

I think you know where this is heading.

Or maybe not. The story of Revenue Collective, and then Pavilion, in the wake of the COVID-19 pandemic has a different arc from some other organizations.

In February of 2020, we were in the midst of planning one of our most ambitious offsites to date. We had a space booked in San Francisco and anticipated 200 Members to be there in person.

Two weeks out, I canceled the event.

At this time, we primarily held in-person events and dinners. We averaged about one virtual event a month. We were built for connection. Connections forged in rooms together. With the news of a deadly virus spreading across the world, I turned back to our values.

Our values have always steered us well. And our number one value is Members first. We needed to put their health and safety above all else. So before any U.S. lockdowns, before toilet paper ran out, before we knew where to buy surgical masks, we canceled our cornerstone offsite.

There were several big name events that were trying to press on or were even still being held. But we stood firm in our values, that Members come before whatever we might have gained from holding the event.

It was the right thing to do, but it was still a terrifying decision. The uncertainty and anxiety we all felt during that time, stressing over our options. We didn't know what would become of our networking community if we couldn't meet in person. We didn't know how long it would be before we could see each other again.

However, in the seed of every crisis is a huge opportunity. I told myself with certainty that this was an opportunity to step up. It was an opportunity to go beyond providing leadership and bring comfort and reassurance to our Members. It was with them in mind that we leapt into action.

And we grew fivefold in 2020.

DOUBLING DOWN ON VALUES

One of the things I love most about working for startups or with a small team is the ability to listen closely and act quickly. It was because of this that we were able to pivot and transform our business to meet our Members' needs in a matter of weeks.

We listened to our Members around the globe. They told us that they were feeling afraid—for their health, for their families, for their livelihoods. So, we acted with generosity, love, and support for our Members.

I began directly connecting with Members, something I still dedicate a majority of my time to doing. We emailed Members more frequently to check in and to share our insights into the market. We ran weekly surveys around topics important to our Members, building a foundation of data, resources, and templates that would become the 1,000+ Knowledge Hub documents our Members have access to today.

We went from one virtual event a month to 25+ virtual events every week, hosting panel discussions, training webinars, happy hours, Q&As with business leaders—anything that would help connect and support our Members.

We leveraged Slack, creating channels not just for business problems, but for Members to share advice with other quarantined parents or those struggling to adapt to working from home.

For our many Members who were furloughed or laid off, we started a new initiative called On the Bench (OTB), which is still one of our most beneficial member programs. Through OTB, Members have access to career coaches, exclusive sessions on interviewing, job searching, and other crucial topics, and connections to vetted talent partners— these are all included in a deck of available candidates that is shared within the membership.

All of this stemmed from a commitment to living our values. We put our Members at the heart of everything we did. We listened to what they needed. We brought more value to their membership without asking for anything in return. We always looked for an opportunity to go above and beyond for our Members. And most importantly, we always came from kindness.

More than anything, we wanted our Members to know that they were not alone in this unpredictable world. We were there to support them through it all.

That sense of support and community was exactly what people needed in a time of isolation, sickness, and fear. The membership applications poured in from all over the world. People craved connection, and we gave them a place to go. We built a place where you could learn, pay it forward, and unlock a new part of yourself. I think that's pretty special.

Special, but it doesn't have to be unique. This is what happens when you develop a strong set of values and use them to guide your decisions. This is what happens when you power your business with generosity. This is what happens when you give more than you get. This is what happens when you come from kindness.

TAKING THE NEXT RIGHT STEP

Revenue Collective changed completely by 2020. We started the year with around 1,000 Members and three full-time employees. By the end, we grew to roughly 3,750 Members and hired 15 more people to join our HQ team.

We took each day one step at a time, taking the next right step down the path of generosity and mutual support. We interviewed each and every new Member and had them buy into our code of conduct, agreeing to give before they get and to not spam their fellow Members. These two simple requests allowed us to build a community where people felt safe asking questions, getting vulnerable about their jobs or their circumstances, and fostered genuine connections.

We taught our Members that offering support and advice is not a cost, but a payment. When you help someone else, you gain a positive reputation. You gain authority. You gain the gratitude of the people you help. This is a path to success. You are not stepping off the path when you take 20 minutes to help someone, even if they don't explicitly do anything in return or even if some people aren't sufficiently grateful. You don't help others for instant gratification. And in this tumultuous time, we all need more support, understanding, and connection.

The more I reflected on the lessons we were teaching our employees and our Members, the more I realized that this philosophy could be applied to so many more people. This idea was bigger than just revenue professionals.

When I started the New York Revenue Collective, then Revenue Collective, it was by operators, for operators. We had a strict no CEO or founder rule. It was a place where embattled executives could go without fear of their discussion making it back to the C-suite. Collective gave the group a feeling of us versus them. That we were in the trenches together, united against our big bad bosses who put too much pressure on us.

At first, it was a safe place to air our grievances. Then, it became a place to help each other learn and grow and win together. Then, it transformed into a large global community united around a shared set of values.

I realized that as we continued to build a world rooted in those values and powered by compassion, that the Revenue Collective name and attitude was less and less aligned with our vision of the world.

We envisioned a world where anyone had the access to the resources they needed to unlock and achieve their professional potential—which is a fancy way of saying there is greatness within all of us and sometimes it just needs a mechanism through which it can be brought forth.

That shouldn't be restricted based on job title or function. The revenue aspect of Revenue Collective was equally mis-aligned. As our community grew and I saw the deep need for such a place in the world, I realized the time for insulation and isolation was over. We needed to be a place for anyone who believed in our values and agreed to adhere to them.

Thus, Pavilion was born.

As I explained to Members, Pavilion sees a world where thousands, and one day millions, of Members, in every city, in every function worldwide, are bound together by a shared sense of support, reciprocity, and belief in long-term relationships.

We see a world where being kind, compassionate, and helpful isn't even altruism. It's not a sacrifice at all—it's the very thing that will propel our success. A world where kind-ness and support are a path to impact, wealth, and content-ment. A world where kind folks finish first.

We believe in the idea that you could pay a simple fee to become part of a supportive community whose sole pur-pose is to help you succeed. Pavilion is a place where we want to help you get where you want to go, unlock the greatness inside of you, and help that greatness see the beautiful light of day.

These ideals are what motivates everyone on the team to come to work every day.

The name itself speaks to a gathering place. Pavilion is a shelter in a tough business world, but one that is open to everyone.

This pivot, and finally accepting that this idea I had could truly make an impact on the broader business world, unlocked new growth levers across the business.

We now have a fully operating CEO Pavilion, structured around noncompetitive cohorts of about 50 people. CEO Pavilion is all about creating that same community support system we had in place for executives, with access to transformational training and coaching and elevated experiences. We are building out this concept for CROs, CMOs, COOs, and maybe one day the entire C-suite.

With the rebrand, we also launched an analyst membership, serving those within their first five years of professional work experience. At this level, providing mentorship and training is crucial to grow the next generation of operators with values of reciprocity and kindness ingrained into every step of their journey.

With the addition of C-level offerings and analyst, there is now a place in Pavilion for every career stage. From top to bottom, we created a safe haven for those who dare to look at business, growth, and success in a new way.

RISING TO THE NEXT CHALLENGE

Since the initial layoffs and lockdowns of the pandemic, the market and the needs of our Members have quickly changed and then changed again. An unprecedented amount of venture capital poured into high-growth startups in 2021. There were more than 1,500 megadeals, roughly double from the previous year, topping out north of $620 billion. New unicorns were formed at a pace of more than 10 per week as the number of private companies valued at over $1 billion increased by nearly 70%.

In a Pavilion study on compensation, we found that executive median on-target earnings grew to more than $325,000 in 2021, an 8.5% climb from the previous year.

Many of our Members were the beneficiaries of all this capital, but with it came more pressure to hit higher and higher growth targets. And ultimately this unfettered growth proved unsustainable with VC funding slowing in early 2022.

At the same time as funding and capital grew, companies faced a huge talent shortage. More than 19 million Americans quit their jobs between April 2021 and September 2021, according to McKinsey. Sales Talent Agency reported that in January 2022, there were 47,000 more sales jobs at startups than people to fill them.

As we saw with funding, the labor market started to swing the other way in early- to mid-2022. Faced with high expectations and hiring challenges, many decided to do what they could with the staff they had. And those who had quit found themselves with less leverage than when they left their jobs.

All of this to say that the past few years have been a tumultuous time for the business world—not to mention all of the other outside factors adding stress and strain to people around the globe. Our world was and will likely continue to be in a state of flux, quickly moving from one side to the other. As soon as we feel like we have a hold on the market, it shifts.

Operating in that uncertainty is extremely difficult for anyone to manage. It's one of the reasons communities have been on the rise. People are craving connections and support to help them figure out the best course of action in this world.

Our values are what allows us to adapt quickly and continue to operate with every change in the market. Were it not for those guide rails, we would have a much more difficult time making decisions, which could be costly—for us and our Members. To rise to the challenges of the modern business world, you need to deeply understand what your business stands for and how you can best provide for your customers every day.

In that same vein, we encourage all of our Members to look at their compensation as a personal framework for aligning with a business and protecting themselves against any market changes that come to pass.

RULES OF COMPENSATION AND NEGOTIATION

Early on in the Revenue Collective days, we drafted an Executive Compensation Bill of Rights for our Members. Compensation is one of the most discussed topics within our community, and Members have told us that our regular compensation studies were crucial in securing the compensation package they've dreamed of.

I drafted these Bill of Rights with one of earliest supporters, Fred Mather, who was a longtime and very successful sales executive with a ton of exits, IPOs, and M&A events under his belt. The point of the Bill of Rights first and foremost was education.

Too many times, people focus on the only thing they can understand when they negotiate—cash. They are scared or intimidated by the rules surrounding securities and tax laws related to equity. They are scared that if they ask for the wrong thing they'll look foolish. They are scared that they have no right to break precedent or to know specific pieces of information.

So we drafted the Bill of Rights to help give people information and, in so doing, to give them confidence, as they headed into these negotiations.

It bears mentioning that when we think about these five key elements, we are not literally referring to rights. This is a negotiating framework. This isn't "Life Liberty and the Pursuit of Happiness." But what it is is a way of thinking about compensation that is broader and more all-encompassing than many people had previously considered. And because it helps people expand their idea about total compensation, it helps provide security to executives whose careers are by definition incredibly volatile. Education and information lead to confidence and security, and this can translate all the way through to your personal life, your ability to be happy at home, a marginal decrease in the amount of stress and worry you carry with you every day.

These principles have literally changed my life and have helped ensure that even in the most difficult times, I've had a lifeline. I've had something, in writing, that was effectively me, from the past, looking out for myself in the future. And so many many times I've thanked that old version of myself. Because that old version of myself was a really good person that cared about me enough to stay in uncomfortable moments and ask for things that are sometimes uncomfortable to ask for, and, months later, those things ended up saving my ass many times over.

I educate our executive Members that they are entitled to five things when it comes to compensation: due diligence, aligned compensation, liquidity, severance, and consulting.

PRINCIPLES OF EXECUTIVE COMPENSATION: ALIGNMENT

Now before we dive into each element I think it's important that we outline the principles here. These principles are very much a part of the overall thesis we're exploring.

The most important principle I try to drill into people's heads when they are thinking about compensation is alignment. Alignment simply means that we want our compensation to align with the outcomes of the company as much as possible. When the investors and founders win, we win. And correspondingly, when they or the company loses, so do we.

This means that, as a principle, we're not trying to get as much as we possibly can to the detriment of the company. That's part of the reason I kept getting fired. Because I was pushing too hard on compensation, which left me out of alignment.

Sure, you can ask for a $400,000 base salary. But when the company is only doing $2 million in total revenue, you are asking for a very significant percentage of the company's revenue to be paid to you. And what you're really doing is making the performance bar you have to clear so high that you are setting yourself up for failure.

I've done thousands of coaching calls with Members over the years, and I remember a marketing executive in New York saying, "Okay, this is great. What else should I get? What else should I ask for?"

I understand the sentiment of course, but that underlying philosophy—that this is a supermarket giveaway and we're trying to run through the aisles and pile as much crap into our carts as possible before the timer rings. That's not the right way to think about it.

The right way to think about it is that when they win, we win. That's all. We are trying to increase the likelihood that when that elusive mistress called Success finally arrives, we are all celebrating in the spoils, not just the lucky few with the foresight.

So let's dive in.

Due Diligence

Due diligence means, executives have the right to adequate time to review the offer—something I strongly suggest doing with a lawyer. There's no better investment you can make than the one you make in yourself, and ensuring that you're accepting an offer that meets your needs is key to setting yourself up for success. Consulting a lawyer is one of the few ways you can be 100% sure you're set up for success.

I remember an email I received a few months ago from my friend Jim (last name redacted and not my most famous friend Jim) saying, "Hey Sam I'm interviewing for a CEO role at a private equity backed company, do you think I should get a lawyer?"

I wanted to reach through my laptop screen and slap him across the face. The most important job in your life, the big time, the role we've all been working so hard toward for decades, and you're wondering if you should have an expert assist you? When the outcome of this negotiation could potentially change your life forever?

I wrote back emphatically, "Yes, you should get a lawyer."

He wrote back, "Okay. Who can you recommend that's relatively cheap?"

This is a perfect example of playing a short small game and not a big long game. Stop trying to save pennies when you're playing for millions. There's that old adage, "There's nothing more expensive than a cheap lawyer." I want you to remember that.

I resisted the urge to reach back through the laptop and smack him a second time (putting the physical impossibilities of that act to the side for the moment) and simply shared that adage and attempted to use the email to shake some sense into him. Hopefully, these few paragraphs can shake some sense into you. If you're an executive and you're interviewing for a big job, get a lawyer, dammit!

The second part of due diligence besides simply being prepared is to arm yourself with questions you can ask to understand more about the company and its prospects. The main thing I want you to remember is simply that you have a right to ask. You have a right to understand a lot about the company you might work for.

And I don't just mean some of the basics of the corporate structure. I mean about the performance of the company specifically. What you are trying to ascertain, fundamentally, when you are performing due diligence is simply how much does the company understand about its position in the market relative to reality. Put another way, has the company set itself up to grow according to its own expectations. Those expectations will be articulated in any number of ways, including how much money it has raised, what the most recent valuation of the company is, whether the salespeople are achieving their quotas, and much more.

But again, the fundamental question is pretty straightforward: Does the market agree with the company's assessment of itself. We provide comprehensive training to perform this due diligence for our Members and go into much greater detail through those trainings, but that's the question at its essence.

Aligned Compensation

This next part might be controversial, but it's something I believe in wholeheartedly. Aligned compensation means that ALL executives are paid on the same bonus structure, even sales executives.

Many organizations will pay the VP of Marketing, for example, 80% base salary and 20% bonus based on reaching certain metrics. Then, they'll pay the VP of Sales a 50/50 structure like an account executive. Paying a sales executive 50/50 puts their focus on cash. That creates resentment within the executive team and can lead to sales executives taking less favorable deals or making other shortcuts that are not in the best interest of the business in order to max out their bonus. The VP of Marketing and the VP of Sales should have the same stake in the business, and be compensated accordingly.

With less of a focus on outright cash, you can align yourself more fully with your organization through liquidity. So when your company makes money, you make money. And vice versa.

This is controversial because the stereotypical perspective is that a sales leader must live with their livelihood on the line to keep them properly motivated. I've been in situations personally when I was pushing hard for a target so I could hit my accelerator at the end of the quarter. I wasn't aligned with the company because my overall compensation was predicated on closing deals in the short term that might not benefit the company in the long term.

I don't believe leaders should be compensated that way. I believe we should be compensated for helping the company achieve its long-term goals whatever they are. And I further believe that the best environment for leadership to do that is one where they don't have an expectation of a near-term injection of cash but assume that it will all come out at the end of the year. I believe people should be able to live comfortably on their base salary so that on a daily basis they can focus on what's best for the business and not worry about taking a vacation or paying rent.

I'd put myself in that situation too many times, and I understood its peril. I remember moving into the West Village into the nicest apartment Camille or I had ever lived in but not doing so from a position of optimism or power but doing so from a nervous comparison-driven position of fear.

It's a terrible feeling to come to work every day worried that on your base salary, you can't afford your lifestyle.

Now, of course, I'm not blaming anyone for my personal predicament. This wasn't anyone's fault. But I know how it feels, and I think it would have been better if the number I built my lifestyle around was the base. If I couldn't afford to live in the West Village and had to, god forbid, live somewhere desolate and soulless like the Upper East Side, well that was life. But focusing on the big number and putting myself in a position where I woke up every day with money on the brain was a terrible way to live.

I encourage you to think holistically about how you might build a company and be aligned with your executive peers, and I will tell you that perhaps the only thing fundamentally great that was built out of fear was survival. But the greatest and best things in the world, in my experience, are built from a sense of purpose and abundance, and that can only come when you're living within your means and are focused on the long term.

Liquidity

When I write "Liquidity" as a right, I mean, as I wrote above, that we have to be focused on equity compensation generally, not that you deserve liquidity in the abstract when others haven't received it.

That said, I give a talk about liquidity to our executive Members all the time. In this case, I'm defining the term "liquidity" as really an allusion to the moment when equity or your ownership stake in a company becomes cash.

THE TWO WAYS TO GET RICH

Now at the beginning of that talk, I typically flash on the screen a picture of a Folgers coffee can. What's the point of that? Well, there are two ways to get rich in my opinion. One of the ways is the way popularized around the country through the puritanical emphasis on thriftiness. Save every day, deprive yourself of simple pleasures, don't spend compulsively, and one day you'll wake up and you'll have saved a lot of money. Even better if you invested it in a diversified portfolio of stocks. Don't go to Starbucks. Make yourself a cup of coffee at home and drink Folgers. Don't have a nice steak dinner with a martini and a delicious shrimp cocktail with that shaved horseradish from St. Elmo in Indianapolis. Cook at home. Stare at the wall. Watch reruns of sitcoms from the eighties. Die alone.

I'm being silly, of course, but you get my point.

The other way to get rich is the way I and every single other person I know has gotten rich. And in that way, every once in a while, every so often, you get an email out of the blue. You fill out a form or two and nearly magically someone wires a shitload of money into your checking account. The company got sold. The company raised a boatload and is offering a secondary sale opportunity. The company paid a dividend.

I can't tell you how many times over the years, that beautiful money machine that was and is GLG would email me out of the blue letting me know they were paying a dividend and here's the amount and please fill out the proper forms with this clearinghouse company.

Elephant Ventures emails me out of the blue, and two months later $25 million arrives in the business checking account, and some portion of that goes into my personal checking account.

Liquidity. Cold hard cash.

The way I've seen people get rich is that they started or own big chunks of very successful private companies and those private companies find a way to generate a return for their shareholders.

And that leads me to the essence of all of this negotiation framework and the essence of the mistake so many of us make when we are negotiating. We focus on the wrong thing. We focus on cash compensation when we should be focused on equity.

CASH COMPENSATION VERSUS OWNERSHIP IN A COMPANY

The problem with cash compensation, to the point of my situation in the West Village in the early part of the twenty-first century, is that you grow into it. I've never seen someone get a huge raise in their base salary and change nothing about their lifestyle.

You had a secondhand Honda. Then you had your own Acura. Then you got a BMW.

You used to go to the Jersey Shore. Then you went to Miami. Then you went to St. Barts.

You used to live in a studio. Then you moved into a big two-bedroom. Then you moved to a big two-bedroom right off the park.

I know that there are plenty of people in the world that get a big raise and don't slowly adjust their lifestyle upward, but I haven't met that many of them. Most folks are like me, at least the ones I know. We get it, we spend it.

And that's the beauty of a big equity stake. You can't spend it. It grows and grows and grows. And then when it arrives, it has the gravity, the mass, to generate really significant returns. Meaningful returns.

A return of 10% a year on $100,000 is great. But 10% a year on $20 million dollars is something else entirely.

And the difference between $20 million and a couple hundred grand is that, unless you're a complete and total moron, you won't be able to adjust your lifestyle quickly enough to overcome the inertia that is the historical rate of return of the public equities market.

So I tell people to focus on equity. Focus on ownership. And that's how you get rich.

Typically, most startup executives receive some allocation of ownership in the company when they start. That allocation is granted as a bucket of stock options that vest over time.

Now, there's a famous phrase in private equity: "Your price, my terms." What that means at its core is that if you want to tell your friends you sold your company for $100 million, go for it, but the terms of the deal will be optimized for the buyer and you might never receive all of that $100 million based on the structure of the deal.

A similar principle applies when you're thinking about equity. You should be focused on the structure of the equity grant just as much as the actual amount of the options. There are a number of terms and conditions that can meaningfully change the probability that the equity, something on paper and theoretical, turns into cash. And because it happens so rarely, we want to maximize those probabilities. We want to do everything we can to increase the chance that the equity becomes cash, and that's where we want to spend our time negotiating.

Some of the liquidity terms I encourage our executives to understand are double trigger, extended exercise, and cashless exercise. We'll review what these mean in the Tactics section at the end of this chapter but the essence and the point is that it's important that you educate yourself on how equity works because true ownership is the best way to generate wealth.

Severance

This is one of the most overlooked aspects of compensation negotiation. As you might remember from earlier chapters, it is because of a 12-month severance payment that I was able to fund Revenue Collective full-time. For more details on negotiating severance, go back to the Chapter 1 tactics.

One point that I didn't mention that is relevant to the basic philosophy is alignment. Severance actually makes you more aligned with your CEO and the executive team. Why? Because if you know you're protected and have a parachute if things go wrong, you'll be much more likely to accept your replacement, advocate for layering where they bring in someone with more senior experience, and generally support the company goals more vocally and proactively. If you're worried about your job security the whole time, you'll be far less likely to advocate for a change in your personal leadership and far more likely to try and sweep things under the rug when there's bad news.

Consulting

Finally, when it comes to the rights of compensation, all executives have the right to consult. Consulting is a nice way to build wealth and protect yourself should you be left without a full-time job.

If you've framed your career the way we talked about earlier in this book, then you will have a wealth of expertise to fall back on. You can, and should, use that hard-earned expertise to make more money.

The tenure for executives at high-growth companies tends to be very short. And it's only getting shorter. With every job I took before Pavilion, I was given less time to solve more challenging problems. Consulting saved me in 2017, and set me up with a new revenue stream where I was in control.

And beyond payment, advising makes you a better C-suite executive. Just like being exposed to other opinions and ideas in a community, advising gives you fresh perspectives and insights into how other people are doing it.

I would proactively request that you have the ability to consult in noncompetitive situations when you're hired as an executive for the above reasons. I think it's reasonable to put some boundaries around the extent of the consulting you might do so that your boss knows you'll be fully focused on your day job and you may even offer to review potential opportunities with them so they feel you're being fair, open, and transparent but I do believe that building a portfolio of revenue streams and opportunities is the only logical conclusion one can draw from declining job tenures across the board.

Rules of Negotiation

Some people love to negotiate. I don't mind it one way or the other, but I draw a lot of strength from being straightforward and direct with my counterparts. I have a few other principles I reference based on years of experience.

The first one is, "Don't bluff." When I was at GLG, I was used to stomping my feet and getting my way as long as I had a powerful executive sponsor. I had developed this perspective that using the phrase "That's not acceptable" was both cool and powerful. During the financial crisis of 2008, my old boss had left, and my new boss was a former peer who, for whatever reason (and I'm sure there were plenty of good ones), didn't like me. At the end of 2009, they gave me a 50% reduction in my pay. It was still north of $300,000 and I was 31 years old so I was doing all right, but it put my lifestyle in jeopardy particularly because I was negotiating a disappointingly acrimonious divorce. When the company cut my pay that much, I trotted out my trusty "That's not acceptable" as a bargaining chip.

I distinctly remember the look on my new boss's face when he said, "Well if that's not acceptable, I'll assume you're resigning, and I'd be happy to accept your resignation."

Bluff called.

I went into a panic because the truth was I needed the money, had no leverage, and no meaningful other options.

The lesson I learned: If you say something isn't acceptable, you better be prepared not to accept it.

So no bluffing. Create situations where there is parity between your choices so that when you say, "That's not acceptable" you really mean it.

As the logical counterpart to no bluffing, I encourage you to firmly and distinctly outline what you are hoping for and what you're willing to accept. Put it down in cold hard numbers. And don't do the bluffing thing. I've been in so many conversations where executives go through a process of articulating their bottom line and then wavering when they receive a number below that bottom line.

If your bottom line is $225,000 base compensation per year and that's your true bottom line, then when the employer offers $200,000 it's very easy to say "No thank you." But if you've never gone to the trouble of specifying these numbers, you'll always be faced with a wave of anxiety and existential angst.

If you decide beforehand and write down both your priorities and the numbers associated with each element of compensation you can go into the negotiation knowing exactly where you stand.

TAKE YES FOR AN ANSWER

And once you do that, you can take yes for an answer. Some people think negotiating itself is a fun exercise. They roll up their sleeves, use feints and counterplays. They imagine themselves in an episode of *Succession* with Brian Cox as

Logan Roy on the other side of the table. They'll use weird words and talk about "landing zones."

But for most of us, time kills deals. Period. The longer it goes on, the less likely the deal will close. And also please remember that everyone remembers the negotiation. People remember you. They remember when you're being a pain in the ass. They remember when they thought the deal was done and you kept coming back with "And another thing."

The best deals are simple deals that progress quickly through the negotiation stage. Be pleasant to work with, say yes when they hit your zone of acceptability between what you want and what you're willing to accept, and focus on the big important items that could potentially change your life.

When you know what you stand for, you can say definitively this is where I draw the line. You'll know what you'll stand firm on in negotiation and where you're willing to compromise.

Compensation shouldn't be about taking as much as you can get. Maybe that's surprising in a section about the rights of compensation, but it shouldn't be if you've read the themes of this book.

You can and should negotiate a compensation package that allows you to provide for yourself and your family. It should protect you in the event of a firing. You should be able to build wealth. However, it's okay to take yes for an answer.

To me, aligning your values and compensation with the organization is what will ultimately bring fulfillment. While this might not result in the highest base salary up front or the best compensation package ever negotiated, it will help you be paid based on your impact on the company and ensure you are working there for the right reasons. It shows you are willing to put in the work and grow with the company. And you should be rewarded for that.

The point is, there will inevitably be many more crises we have to navigate in our lifetimes, most of which will impact our ability to work in some capacity. But remember that in every crisis, there is an opportunity to help someone else. You can set yourself up for security during uncertain times, but don't forget about others. If we all took a little time every day to help someone, I truly believe the world would be a happier place. It's what we're working toward in Pavilion.

So as this narrative inches closer to the time I am writing this book, I have one final lesson for you. It's about reaching the ultimate destination—happiness.

CHAPTER 7 TACTICS: UNDERSTANDING EQUITY: TERMS YOU SHOULD KNOW

Negotiating compensation packages that include structured payments over the long term, rather than up-front cash, will help protect you in uncertain markets and better align you with company goals. These are a few of the key terms I've found crucial to negotiating such a package.

Double Trigger

Some people assume that when the company gets sold your unvested options immediately vest and you can turn them into equity and sell them at the acquisition price. But, no, that's not what happens. In fact, if you're not careful, your unvested equity might get wiped out completely.

"Double trigger" is a phrase you can insert into your employment agreement to help protect you and increase the likelihood that your equity becomes cash. The phrase refers to the idea that "triggers" are events in the company lifecycle.

In this case, the first "trigger" would be a change of control, meaning the company got sold.

Now that might not be enough for your unvested options to vest. And maybe they shouldn't. If we're focused on alignment, it's not clear to me that it's fair that you immediately have every incentive to leave the company. And it frankly makes you less attractive to the acquiring entity.

Okay, fair enough.

But something that happens is that a company gets bought and the acquirer looks at all the redundancies that are there. They say, "We don't need two sales teams and two finance teams and two marketing teams. We can improve efficiency by getting rid of the extra people."

And that, my friends, is the second trigger.

So bringing it all back home, to quote an old poet from Minnesota, double trigger is when your company gets sold and something happens to you such that you're out of a job. Those two triggers in sequence would then vest your unvested equity, and you'd be able to sell your stock even if there was a significant amount that was unvested.

Double trigger language needs to be comprehensive, specific, and the percent of unvested equity to accelerate should be 100%.

One important little point that we coach our executives on—make sure it's not just getting fired that's the second trigger. Because there are all kinds of games companies play that aren't technically firing but could completely mess up your life. They could say, "Well we're not firing you, Sally, but our headquarters are in Saskatoon, Canada. So unless you want to move you and your family and pets to Canada, I guess you're quitting and we're not firing you."

So the language for double trigger should refer not just to firing but "a material change in job responsibility or geography." That should be comprehensive enough to tackle any meaningful eventuality.

Extended Exercise Period

Increasing the amount of time you have to exercise your options when you leave a company from a standard 90 days to 12 months or more gives you the opportunity to evaluate the company over a longer time frame before deciding what to do with your equity. In fact, 70% of executive Members surveyed in 2022 had an exercise period over 12 months, with 30% having an exercise period over 2 years.

Typically, options expire 90 days after you leave your company, so you either need to exercise them, which means write a big check, or they evaporate. The problem as I write this in 2022 is that it's a double whammy, because you actually have to pay "income" tax on the implied gain between the stated valuation and the price you pay for the shares. This is a bit of insanity because you haven't actually made any money, especially if it's a tiny company without compelling near-term prospects. The taxes you pay are typically at least double what you might pay to exercise and could be way way more if the company has been aggressively fundraising.

Imagine a situation where the company has just raised a bunch of financing on growth targets they can't hit. Maybe that's even the reason you're fired. So now there's this massive valuation out there, and the company is likely going to have to lower the valuation in recognition they were overly optimistic but you paid taxes on the full amount of the optimism. It's a shitty situation, and one I've personally been in.

So if you can, ask for longer than 90 days to exercise your shares. I recommend two years as a fair number that gives you enough time to evaluate the performance of the company without it being an undue burden on your employer.

With all of these lessons in mind, there is still one thing missing that will help you unlock your full potential. It's what helped me rise to the challenge of the pandemic and show up with love, empathy, and compassion for our Members. And that was love for myself.

CHAPTER 8

The Last Piece of the Puzzle: Leading with Love

Backing up to the end of 2019, I was professionally in the place I always wanted to be. We were still called Revenue Collective, and we were growing. More and more people were buying into a world where values and generosity were at the root of decision making. We were building the foundation on which we could scale. We were making a difference.

But despite that professional success, my personal life was far from thriving. I won't go into too much detail, but I separated from my wife Camille in late 2019. I finally found what I was looking for in the corporate world, but, ultimately, I was lost.

I took a lonely trip to Florida that year, hoping to find some peace and decompress from the personal stress. It turns out Miami is not the place you should go for relaxation. I ended up spending my time there miserable and frustrated.

Yet, on a rooftop at the One Hotel in Miami in December 2019 I had one more epiphany. A personal one to mirror the professional epiphany I had at the rest stop back in 2017. I was sitting there nursing a drink, spending the holidays alone and feeling sorry for myself. That's when I finally began to really analyze myself and who I wanted to be.

For me, mindset begins with the narrative inside my head. That voice that sits on top of my perceptions and applies commentary and critique to everything happening in my life.

For so many years, that voice was not very pleasant. Throughout my life, I had a longstanding Google Doc filled with goals and resolutions. And reading through it, one would get the distinct sense that I don't like myself very much. My inner commentary was like a really tough athletic coach or a disapproving parent who is never happy with anything and has a problem with every accomplishment. Why wasn't it better? Why wasn't it more? Why wasn't that an A+?

I think about that inner voice like an aquifer. In fact, it's almost your inner essence is the aquifer. Your primordial view of the world and yourself in it. Your feelings and emotions pass through that aquifer to form words.

Those thoughts form your words, who you think you are. That flow becomes your essential feelings about how you look at the world. Suddenly that inner voice holds real power and can influence how you move through life.

And it determines whether you look at your life from a place of fear and pain, or from a place of love and abundance. All of your rationalizations stem from these fundamental belief systems that have already put the words in place.

And that's why it's like an aquifer. If your inner thoughts are already tainted with self-doubt and loathing, then your words, feelings, and actions will be tainted, too. Changing yourself is incredibly hard because you have to go back before you can move forward. You have to dispense with all of these fundamental ideas you might have about yourself. All of these things that you think are objective facts. You need to realize that they aren't set in stone, and that you might be looking for a reason to bring tension or frustration or pain or anger into a relationship or into dynamics because of how you talk to yourself. That's what I had done most of my life.

I can't stress this enough because this is very, very difficult to practically accomplish. This is foundational. Your idea that you are who you are. That they are who they are.

I remember a friend of mine once asking me, "What if everything was perfect? What if your life was absolutely perfect, including your relationships?"

I laughed when he said that. It couldn't possibly be true. Obviously, there were all kinds of problems. And all kinds of problems that other people had. They weren't my problems. They were their problems. I was beset with their challenges. Even though I was also a failure and couldn't get anything right.

My coach, John, calls these thoughts and ideas "your paradigm." Your existing mental map of who you are and who everyone else is. And the problem with your paradigm is that it's very smart. It's you after all. It's logical. It's persuasive. It's all of the things you are but with a particular view of the world.

It was there on the rooftop in Miami when I thought back to that run with my friend Scott, the one who helped me emerge from the sense of failure when I was fired in 2017. The one who told me how unhelpful it is to be so hard on yourself.

Carrying around all of these burdens and expectations and feelings of inadequacy doesn't create the right framework or energy to spur new opportunities, and, perhaps just as importantly, it doesn't make other people want to be around you very much.

So I thought to myself, How can I make the same changes I made professionally, personally? How can I power myself with generosity and give myself some grace? The answer was I needed to learn to love myself. I needed to be the kind of person I would actually want to spend time with as a friend. I needed to show myself some compassion.

BREAKING THE CYCLE OF SELF-LOATHING

As someone who struggles with and is treated for depression, I had been in therapy for years. But I was never sure if it was working. I would go in and talk about my relationships and leave those sessions more embittered and embattled then I'd been before.

For me, some of that came from the inherent nature of therapy to look backwards. My therapist would help me look back on the causes of my pain, find who or what could be responsible, and then validate my feelings based on my past experiences.

While probably not my therapist's intention, I would come out of my therapy sessions blaming others for my problems. It wasn't me, it was how I was raised. Or because of some experience. It would affirm that I was right, and it was others in my life who were in the wrong. That made me less willing to compromise and centered my experience in an ultimately detrimental way.

I have a theory that every therapist wants you to get divorced. That's, of course, very problematic, but I just remember so many times going into those sessions and either explicitly or implicitly asking the question, "I'm not crazy, right? That person is objectively messed up." And of course my shrink would rarely ever directly say, "Yes they're messed up. You're right and they're wrong." But it was strongly implied. And there was one time I was complaining, and he literally said, "I just want you to know, that's messed up, and, no, you're not crazy."

Well, as someone who didn't want to get divorced again, who was looking for a way to repair my relationship, and who wanted to have harmonious relationships with people in my life, it's not particularly useful to walk out of every therapy session fired up and ready to have an argument because my indignation was just validated.

I remember for years and years and years, asking Camille, "Do I seem different? Is it working?" My experience is this: If you literally can't tell if something is working after years and years and years, that's because it's not working. There's not some mysterious force at play that's subtly shaping you into a saint but you can't tell. You'll know when it's working. And if you're worried something isn't working, it's because it isn't.

I began seeing executive coach John Mark Shaw in October of 2019, and he brought a new perspective to me. That perspective was about positivity and a forward-looking view of the world.

John's perspective is a common one shared by all kinds of people throughout history from Napoleon Hill, to Tony Robbins, to Oprah. It's based on the idea that we are infinitely powerful spiritual beings and that if we focus intently on good and positive things, good and positive things will happen to us.

I realized on the Miami rooftop that therapy wasn't working for me—but coaching was. Most importantly, beneath all of that, I realized I needed to start loving myself. I needed to say it out loud. I needed to hold myself in much greater regard. And if I did that, everything would change.

And it did.

I can't tell you how I knew. I just knew. I knew that love was the secret that needed to be unlocked. I began typing furiously into my phone. I have that long rambling message even today. I remember literally crying at that bar when I wrote "You are not a disappointment. You have nothing to be ashamed of. You are wonderful and beautiful and I am so proud of you."

The light bulb, the epiphany, was that I needed to directly speak to myself and support myself. Because I had carried around so much disappointment and shame. Because I was scared that I wasn't worthy. Because I was afraid to be happy and afraid to be mediocre.

The practice, the last piece of the puzzle, was love. And maybe that sounds silly. But it's real. If you can hold yourself in high regard, not out of egotism, but because you are worthy and valuable and beautiful. If you can practice doing that, and repeating it daily, it will change your life.

Following that trip to Florida, I channeled my inner Stuart Smalley. I started telling myself directly, both out loud and in writing, that I loved myself. More than three years later, that is still a part of my daily journaling practice. I don't just journal my gratitude or thanks, but I write directly to myself with compassion and care and say "I love you, Sam." I write "I am so proud of you. I even talk to myself a lot particularly when I'm working out a difficult challenge.

We all assume that the voice in our head is speaking complete sentences. And it's not. It's speaking half sentences. It's a few words here and there and some feelings and some images. And that's why actually writing out how you feel and talking to yourself out loud is so useful. Because it forces you to put these ideas into actual words and think in complete sentences.

Fear is many people's dominant emotion. I know it was mine for much, much too long. I was so overly focused on negativity, on what I didn't have, on what wasn't there, instead of what I did have. I was so stressed about the future, so focused on my every flaw and failing. When I started writing and speaking to myself with compassion, I realized I could put that fear aside. I realized there was nothing to be afraid of.

My advice to you is to confront the fear, confront the impulses. Confront your inner voice. Dig as deep as you can to reset your aquifer and figure out who you want to be.

Only then can you find what you love and do it. All of the business lessons in this book are useful, but they lack vigor and impact if you are missing the fundamental ingredient of self-love.

FRAMING YOUR FUTURE

Embracing self-compassion and working with John Mark Shaw completely changed the trajectory of my life. One of things I loved about working with him, and with other executive coaches, was the optimistic, forward-looking lens with which they taught me to view the world.

One of my favorite exercises centered around building scaffolding images when goal setting. I find that there is a fundamental issue in how a lot of people set their goals. Most people list goals with theoretical language, saying things like "I hope that I will do X" or "My goal is to achieve Y." I've learned that this is how you introduce doubt and ultimately set yourself up for failure.

Through coaching, I found that goals should be set as if you have already accomplished them. Imagine yourself in the future looking back on what you've already done. Write a paragraph of where you are at the end of the quarter, a year in the future, or even five years from now. Add as many details as you can. This is the trick. It needs to feel as real as possible. That's the scaffolding-images part. You are creating a clear picture in your mind that will help support you in accomplishing your goals.

So set the scene for yourself. Use specific details: Where are you? What's the weather outside? What specifically were you just doing before you sat down to write your reflections?

From there, list out specific accomplishments, how you accomplished them, and how good they made you feel. Use positivity. Here's one of mine:

"It's December 2022. I'm sitting in my living room enjoying a drink while snow falls gently outside and my dogs sleep happily by my feet. I'm so happy and grateful that two months ago I handed out physical copies of my book to Pavilion members at our in-person conference. I did it by hiring a book coach, recruiting my colleague Kerri to help draft the manuscript based on my outline and interviews, and signing a publishing contract with Wiley. I am ecstatic to be a published author and chart the course for a kinder way to do business."

Do you see how this is so much more powerful than saying "I hope to publish a book someday"? As we talked about in the previous chapter, abundance begets abundance. When you approach your life and your work with positivity, optimism, and abundance, that is exactly what you will get in return from the universe. When you frame your goals in this way, you'll be surprised by how much quicker you will achieve them. This is all about setting yourself up for success and opening your mind to the generosity of the universe.

In Pavilion, we offer dozens of schools and courses that can help you level up or hone a particular skill. The cornerstones of Pavilion University are the first two programs we ever built—CRO School and Rising Executives School. We begin both programs with a workshop on framing your career. In the modern world, there's no linear path to career growth. Each career is a sequence of non-linear leaps from one opportunity to the next. Which makes framing your career all the more important.

We teach how having a detailed career plan helps you work backwards to understand sequential steps along your journey, exactly as I learned in my goal-setting exercise with John Mark Shaw. This isn't to say your career can't or won't take other paths, but if you have a destination in mind, it makes difficult decisions (e.g., Should I take this new job? Should I move to this new region?) easier if you understand the general direction in which you want to move.

Framing your career requires self-reflection and self-compassion. Maybe where you wanted to go before isn't where you want to go now. That's okay. Reset your destination and work backwards. A Pavilion Member told me that for years she had one destination in mind—CRO. But when I challenged several Members to build out their five-year plan, she started to question herself. What really drove her pursuit of that title? What was it that she actually wanted out of her career? Did she need to be a CRO to get the freedom that she craved? She said she felt that too often salespeople are chasing the next accelerator. Feeling like the position they hold isn't good enough. That you need more. But when you get there are you happy?

This really struck me. I spent years in that cycle, letting frustrations simmer. I was stuck, resenting what others had and comparing it to what I didn't have. It felt like nothing I did would ever be enough. I thought I had to get to the next level to get what I wanted. To attain that wealth and status and respect I craved. To finally feel that I was living up to my potential.

Ultimately she found that what drove her was the power to choose who she led and how and in what ways she would lead. With that framing in mind, she could turn back to the task of identifying how she could make that a reality.

My roadside epiphany in 2017 set me on a path that ultimately led to self-compassion and a new way to think about what it means to be successful. Like this Member, I had to get to the heart of what I wanted. To the heart of the fear that led me to be dissatisfied. To really understand myself and what I wanted. Only then, could I build the foundations for a new kind of life and a new kind of business.

It flows from playing for the long term, as we discussed in Chapter 2. It's also reminiscent of the OKR structure of goal setting. In this framework, you state your intended end objective, like being promoted to VP of Sales. Then, you list three to four key results you need to achieve to accomplish this objective. In this case, that could be $10 million in new business closed, presenting three opportunities to the board, and hiring an inside sales team before the end of the year.

Like many startups, we use the OKR framework in Pavilion HQ. And if we achieve 100% of our OKRs, we know they weren't ambitious enough. We want to keep pushing ourselves to see what's possible. To see how much we can get by giving all we have. To see the future before us and find a way to get there. Having compassion for our Members and ourselves is how we are able to do just that.

EMBRACING POSITIVITY

Many have written about the impact of positivity on achieving your goals. An article I like is from Arthur Brooks, published in *The Atlantic* in December 2020. Brooks talks about John Norcross, a psychology professor at the University of Scranton. Norcross analyzed both successful and failed New Year's resolutions, noting the behaviors with both. He found that resolution failure is associated with negative thinking, such as focusing on the harm from the old behavior, berating yourself for slipping up, wishing that the challenge didn't exist in the first place, and minimizing the threat.

Breaking from this cycle and framing your future with positivity is the first step in actually getting where you want to go. The perception of your reality will ultimately prove true. If you've attended one of my sessions on executive compensation and negotiation, you might have heard me joke about 60/40 relationships. In any relationship, you should always feel that you are giving more than you are getting. You'll know you're doing it right if the scorekeeping part of your brain keeps nagging you that you're putting in more than you're getting out.

It's the key to a good marriage and a good working relationship. Pavilion was founded on this give-to-get principle. This book is about conducting business from a place of generosity. Positive framing falls in line with this train of thought.

I'm not saying you won't have negative thoughts or that you shouldn't be realistic about your situation, whatever it may be. Anyone who works with me knows I'm prone to moodiness and can be direct. But what I am saying is that if you put positive thinking into the world without expectation of getting back all, or any, of what you gave, you will end up reaping the rewards.

The power of self-compassion, positivity, and leading with love were the final puzzle pieces in the framework I had been building since the start of Revenue Collective. Now that I unlocked this part of myself I could finally look to the future with optimism—both professionally and personally.

My goals going into 2020 were simple. Every day I wanted to write, read, exercise, be kind to others, and be kind to myself.

That fundamental framework initially felt strange and alien, but the essence is that I was shifting from being a punitive disciplinarian constantly frustrated by my inconsistency to being a supportive parent and coach who held myself and my ambition in unconditional positive regard.

To this day, I still use this framework. I have what I call a good day sheet, and the markers of a good day are the same as my goals for 2020. If I was able to journal, read, exercise, and help someone else, then I had a good day. No matter what else happened, if I can check each of these habits off, the day was a success. It's an objective way to take a step back and make small, incremental steps toward happiness.

Notice that these daily goals are not hyper-specific. My goal of daily exercise is not saying that I need to run 20 miles or burn a certain number of calories. A 20-minute jog counts. So does a half marathon. I could write five pages in my journal, or I could write one word. It matters more that I did something, whatever it may be. And it matters more that I don't beat myself up for not doing the absolute most every day.

And the results speak for themselves. I'm happier, my business has grown, and my life is exceeding my wildest dream since I started embracing positivity, abundance, and generosity.

LOVE IS A LEAP OF FAITH

How can you play for the long term if you're not guaranteed success? How can you trust that all your efforts will pay dividends? How can you believe that the lessons of this book will actually work?

Here's what I've discovered.

All wonderful things are leaps of faith. In some way, you have to simply trust that if you put the work in and you approach life with optimism, gratitude, and abundance, that things will work out. You have to believe that. Even when it's hard.

All wonderful things are wonderful precisely because they are not guaranteed. I want to go back to the person I was getting fired from GLG or go back to the sad and broken kid who didn't get into Thomas Jefferson, or Princeton, or the Echols Program at UVA, the kid that felt like a failure.

I want to go back and tell that kid everything will be all right, everything will work out great.

But if I did tell myself that, if I could find some way to travel back in time, there's the reality that I might not have achieved any of this.

Because that's the whole point. If things were predestined, if they were guaranteed, there wouldn't be any fear, there wouldn't be any risk.

And that's exactly the opposite of how things need to be to work out. There needed to be risk. There needed to be failure. There are no guarantees. As much as I'd like to go back in time and tell my younger self, "Here's what your retirement account will look like in your mid-forties, so chill" it's doubtful that would have worked.

You have to trust. You have to believe. Not because it's guaranteed but precisely because it's not. You have to step off the cliff and trust you'll be caught with your heart full.

And in that way, so many of the lessons of this book are quasi-spiritual. I'm not telling you to go to church every Sunday (although you can if you want), but I am telling you that you have to figure out a way to fill your heart with belief and power your contentment from inside. And that if you can do that and take that leap, you'll be amazed at what you're capable of accomplishing.

The key, again, and to reiterate, is using positivity and love to power that belief, not fear and anxiety.

THE HOUSE IN THE HAMPTONS

I want to tell you a little story about the power of future-casting and the power of taking a leap of faith and believing in yourself. And I'm sure there are cynics out there armed with the regular "This is not statistically significant" counterpoint.

But nevertheless.

It was the beginning of the pandemic. I had a handful of employees and about $180,000 in the business checking account. Summer was approaching, and I'd been cooped up in the apartment for a long time.

If you've ever spent a summer in New York, you know that it's best to get out of the city when the heat arrives, if you can afford to. The streets smell like urine and poop. Garbage is rotting. It becomes oppressively humid.

And the place most New Yorkers want to go is the Hamptons on the east end of Long Island. Now, the Hamptons are incredibly expensive. Hard to say if it's worth it; that's up to you. But for me, it's a beautiful place and one I love spending time in.

However, I knew that if I rented a place I wanted a pool, and I wanted it to be nice. I was tired of getting the cheap, shitty place and feeling self-conscious and keenly aware of the lack of things like a place to swim or air conditioning.

I found a beautiful home with a pool and all the things I wanted. And to rent it for the months of July and August was a whopping $70,000. A huge amount of money.

I spoke to John, my coach, and he said, "What if you think of this as an investment in the future? What if you make a resolution to yourself to 10x the investment? What if by being in this amazing, beautiful place for an extended period of time you come up with some ideas so powerful that they catapult your business into the next stratosphere?"

Well, that sounded compelling to me, and it reinforced my own desires anyway. So I said okay. I wired the money from the business account (at that time before we had investors the business account and my personal lifestyle were hopelessly intertwined as most family businesses are). This was a full half of the money available to me and by all accounts a stupid and feckless decision. I immediately had a panic attack.

"You stupid f***ing idiot. You can't have $5 in the bank without finding a way to blow it. You reckless imbecile."

My inner voice had reared its head. My paradigm. It was chastising me as it had for so many years. If Camille had been around, I would have found a way to blame her, I'm sure, or picked some other kind of fight.

I called John back and said, "I think I just made a terrible mistake."

"Calm down, Sam. Remember, we talked about this. This is an investment. This is just your paradigm trying to keep you in common hour thinking. Focus on the 10x. Focus on the joy of being out there."

I talked myself off a ledge and resolved to make this a 10x decision.

When I got there, the house was as beautiful as I'd imagined. I swam in the pool every day. I hung out on the deck and watched the lavender grow. I went to the beach and cooked steak and read *Norwegian Wood* by Murakami and watched *The Expanse* on television. I had a blast and began to rebuild my relationship with Camille as well. I hired Carly Pallis, our first VP of Marketing, and Laura Guerra, our first VP of Sales.

I remember feeling happy and relaxed and having a lot of fun.

And come October, when I logged into the business checking account, lo and behold there was $700,000 in there. We had 10x'ed our membership. It was really amazing. By the end of the year, we'd broken through $1,000,000 in the checking account.

Now, 18 months later, I've seen millions of dollars in both my and the business account numerous times. But back then, that was the first time I'd ever seen a million dollars. It was some mythical barrier I had never truly believed I was capable of crossing. And it had been crossed.

Powered, in part, by a leap of faith, and a resolution to believe in the power of abundance, optimism, and transformation.

CHAPTER 8 TACTICS

Practice Writing Out "I Love You"

I derive a lot of value from writing down "I love you" in my journal almost every day. I journal out a couple of paragraphs of observations about the day, things I've done or thought about. But I always end by writing, "I love you, Sam." The first time I did it on the roof of the One Hotel, I felt simultaneously silly and like I'd had a major breakthrough.

I knew I was on to something because I knew that's what had been missing. My own efforts to be a better friend to myself. That is truly when things began to change.

And, as with all things, practice helped reinforce these ideas. Over the course of 2020, I journaled nearly every day. I journaled when all of New York City shut down. I journaled when Trump got COVID. I journaled when the election was finalized. And in each of those entries I would end with "I love you, Sam. I'm so proud of you."

When people used to ask me if I was happy, I would never be sure. But now I am. It took a lot of practice. And it took a willingness to feel silly and specifically talk to myself. But it has fundamentally changed my self-image and my perception of who I am.

Give it a shot.

CHAPTER 9

Arriving at Happiness

Before 2017, I wasn't sure that I could ever arrive at true happiness. The gnawing feeling of unrealized potential and frustration that ate away at me most of my life made happiness feel out of reach. It wasn't in the cards for someone like me.

If only I had been able to see a little further down the road. That there was a turn ahead that would change everything. An exit ramp to a new life and a sense of fulfillment in what I get to do every day. A new destination driven by values, generosity, and helping others get what they want out of their careers, and their lives.

It's sometimes still hard to believe in 2022. But this vision we have at Pavilion is proof that this kind of business works. That you can leverage this strategy and build a successful life yourself. That you don't need to step on someone else to get to the top. That there's room for all of us around a big table to contribute what we know and learn from the person next to us.

Backing up to December of 2020, the decision I made to embrace self-compassion spurred real changes in my life. Camille and I reconciled, and I'm happy to say we are together today, embarking on a new adventure to fulfill Camille's entrepreneurial dreams.

I have taken leaps of faith several times since 2017, but the biggest one was challenging my self-beliefs and committing to be happy. Truly happy.

The Untethered Soul by Michael Alan Singer has had a profound impact on me, coupled with all of the lessons I've espoused in my own book. In it, Singer writes that you have to make the commitment that you will be happy without exception.

In addition to my wife, my dogs, and my work, I find the greatest happiness in running. I love to run. It saved me during my difficult first divorce and has seen me through all the ups and downs in my life. But if something happened to me tomorrow where I could no longer run, I know now that I will still be happy. I am committed to being happy.

You don't have to be happy every second of every day. There will always be times of strife or where you just can't see what there is to be happy about. But like embracing self-compassion, positivity, and journaling, it's a practice. It's a commitment to find joy in your life.

In this regard, I often think of my dog Oswald. When we adopted him, he already had a leg partially amputated. But you would never know it by the way he runs around or wags his tail. Imagine feeling that kind of unbridled happiness, despite whatever life brings.

Arriving at happiness is a choice you can make. I believe we all have control over our lives. There's a better world awaiting you if you believe that. It's spiritual in a way. It really is putting faith in the universe that it will take care of you. It's that abundance mindset that every positive, happy, helpful thing you do will come back to you. And even if we're wrong and there's no free will, it's more fun to think that way anyway.

VALIDATING OUR WORK

So as I actively chose happiness, compassion, and kindness, I received one more validation that this life path was working for me—and my business.

In February of 2021, an investor from Elephant Ventures, Peter Fallon, reached out inquiring about the state of the business. We'd been in touch briefly the year before, and he'd heard some good things about us.

For my part, there were a few minutes when I debated even answering the email. There is precious little about Elephant online. And I didn't really need another tiny little investor offering us $1 million and acting like it was some kind of groundbreaking amount of capital. But I have a rule I like to adhere to when people email you offering you lots of money:

"Take every call."

So we got on the Zoom, and I walked him through the business and the growth. I'm an open book when it comes to discussing business performance. To the point of "play a long big game," I don't really see the percentage or relative gain in being too coy. Our numbers aren't our plan, and even if you had our plan you'd still have to execute it, and even then there's so much soul in this business that you'd still have to be me.

So I shared very openly with Peter. I told him of our plans to rebrand to Pavilion (we officially rebranded in June 2021) and what I thought that would mean for the business.

He was intrigued and said, "If you're willing to send me last year's financials, I'd be happy to give you a read on valuation."

Well, I had no real idea what Revenue Collective was worth and had just had an annoying conversation with my friend Hugh, in which he told me the company would trade at "1 to 1.2 times revenue," which basically meant a company that grew fivefold during a pandemic would be worth its revenue.

So yes, I would like a read on valuation if you please.

I sent over our 2020 results. Peter wrote back fairly quickly, "Are you willing to send by quarter?"

And to the point of competitive differentiation, the reason that he was being so elliptical and measured in his approach was that so many founders can only think transactionally about sharing information. They are short-term focused and don't understand that value creation is not a game of one-hit wonders. You have to show up every single day for a very long time, but at some point that long time will have passed, and then good things might happen.

So yes, I can use Quickbooks well enough to figure out how to send over our results by quarter. I sent those over, and he innocently asked, "Are you free this Friday to chat?"

I logged on to the Zoom that Friday with my heart beating. I was alone in a one-bedroom apartment with Walter sleeping in his orange bed at my feet and Oscar in the blue bed. I was working on the same laptop I'd bought for myself in 2015 when I was fired and resolved to only use my own machine going forward. I was barefoot.

Peter said, "Well we think the company is worth $80 million. We want to invest $25 million with a certain amount going straight to you and the balance going into the company."

I can share the play-by-play even years later because this was a life-changing moment for me. One that will have altered the trajectory of my life forever.

After a few additional conversations, I signed a Term Sheet bringing in support from GTM Fund—an early-stage venture fund backed by 165+ Go-To-Market leaders, many of whom are Pavilion Members. We spent the month of March in due diligence, and the deal closed in early April of 2021.

In the past, I had politely declined investor interest in Revenue Collective. One reason for this was I wasn't ready to be beholden to a board. As we discussed at length in Chapter 1, I was never very good at working for someone else. Revenue Collective was the project that saved me and unlocked a brand-new life. What I loved most about it was that the HQ team was building it alongside our Members. It was made for operators by operators. I didn't want a group of investors to change that dynamic.

Another reason I declined funding initially was frankly because we didn't need it. Revenue Collective, and even now as Pavilion, had always operated at break even. We weren't burning capital. Because of that, we grew perhaps more slowly than we could have, but controlling our growth in the early stages is what allowed us to really get to know our Members and what value looked like to them. It helped us flesh out this idea and get it off the ground.

So what made this investment offer different? Well, there were a few reasons.

Following our rapid growth during the pandemic, it was beyond clear that this community was filling a huge gap in the market. And if we really wanted to see where this idea could take us, a cushion would be good. It seemed like the perfect time to truly take off.

In early 2021, we had two learning programs—CRO School and Rising Executives School. Both were wildly popular among our Members and proved there was an appetite for structured learning in our community. The $25 million funding meant we could expand our course offerings quickly. When we unveiled the Pavilion brand to the world that June, we also announced 13 Pavilion

University programs, covering sales, marketing, customer success, and revenue operations, with almost all included at no additional cost for our Members. By the end of 2022, we'll have launched more than 50 Pavilion University programs across all functions and membership tiers.

The funding also aided in our acquisition of two communities—SDRDefenders, which became the bedrock of the Analyst membership tier, and FinOps, our first foray into non–revenue-generating functions. It's the first step in our dream of being a community where all can realize and get the resources they need to achieve their professional potential.

We also invested heavily in building our Member Success Team, ensuring that all of our Members were heard and supported, and got the value they wanted out of their membership.

So when we were approached by Elephant, the time was right from a business perspective and a personal one. Not only did the investment validate all of the work I'd been doing on the business and myself, but it created generational wealth for me and my family—a culmination of so much hard work.

And it came to pass, not when I was grinding my gears in negativity and frustration, but when I had finally learned to embrace compassion and generosity as the core of my life and my business. It came at a time where I was ready to leap into the great unknown, understanding that the universe would provide more to those who brought love, kindness, and positivity into the world.

This funding set up the future of Pavilion and allowed us to bring our mission even further.

LOOKING TO THE FUTURE

As of May 2022, the valuation of Pavilion is more than $200 million with 8,500 Members in 50 chapters around the world—from New York City to Singapore to Oslo to Brazil.

By the time this book goes to print, we expect to have 10,000 or more Members. I truly believe that one day there will be a world where hundreds of thousands, maybe even millions, of people buy into the belief that generosity and kindness is the way to do business. Pavilion Members will lead this charge and make transformational changes at their organizations around the world.

We will continue to bring this idea, this framework to as many people as we can. Imagine a world where it isn't dog eat dog. Where you could trust that everyone was operating in good faith and there was a seat at the table for anyone who wanted one. Maybe you think that's naive, but Pavilion and its Members are proof that it can happen. They are proof that coming from kindness is not just a nice thing to do, but a long-term strategy that will help you reach your goals and help others along the way.

We envision a world where you don't have to go it alone. A world where you have a global community cheering you on and is actively vested in your success. At Pavilion, we will continue to build the resources our Members tell us they need. We will listen closely, then take the next right step to act quickly. And then the next right step after that. Again and again until we are running. Until this idea, this concept is in every corner of the globe and in every board meeting.

At its heart, this idea is simple. Look to help others before you help yourself. Do as much as you can for other people and ask nothing in return. Try as hard as you can to stop keeping score. Play a long big game instead of a short small game. Build relationships not transactions. And try to use the power of love, optimism, and gratitude to power as much of your decision making as possible.

In the early days, I didn't allow myself to think that this simple idea was also a big idea. That the framework I put forth through a dinner group could resonate with so many people. Even as I finally stepped up to work full time on this project, I was happy to just get us to 2,000 people.

I sometimes still can't believe that I get to go to work every day and help someone. It's more than I ever could have dreamed for myself.

I spend the majority of my time talking with Members. They send me emails and messages or call me up to tell me about their struggles, both at work and in their personal lives. They share the things they love about Pavilion—and what could use improvement. And I listen to each and every one of them and try to give my best advice. That advice usually boils down to everything I've talked about in this book. Embracing kindness, consideration, reciprocity, and a sense of spirituality powered by love will unlock doors. It will help you get to where you want to go.

My life changed when I realized all you need to do is listen and give people what they are asking for. I didn't need to keep score or make a mental tally of every slight. I could help others without expectation and play a long game that would give me so much more at the end of the day.

Every stumbling block along the way built the foundation on which Pavilion now stands. From my realization at the rest stop to the exit ramp that showed me a new way was possible. I reset my destination, fueling my journey with generosity and used my values as the compass. I embraced self-compassion as the last piece of the puzzle and found opportunities to help people through crises big and small.

The old adage of "nice guys finish last" is wrong. Business is not zero sum. Nice people can succeed in business and in life. Kind folks can finish first.

I have just done it, and you can too.

ABOUT THE AUTHOR

Sam Jacobs is the founder and CEO of Pavilion. He launched Pavilion as Revenue Collective in 2016 and bootstrapped the company to $10 million in annual recurring revenue before taking on a $25 million growth financing round in early 2021, led by Elephant Ventures and GTM Fund.

Prior to Pavilion, Sam spent 15 years as a senior revenue leader at VC-backed companies in the New York area including Gerson Lehrman Group, Axial, Livestream/Vimeo, The Muse, and Behavox.

He lives in the West Village of Manhattan with his wife and two dogs, William and Oswald, and mourns the passing of his beloved Walter in the summer of 2022.

INDEX

Price Is Right (TV show), 141
Pride, 18–20
Princeton University, 17, 197
Principles, *see* Values
Private equity, 172
Private spaces, 115
Product-market fit, 24, 127, 131–132
Promotions, 149–150
"Pulling the thread," 105–106

R

Real Housewives of Atlanta
     (TV show), 58
Reciprocity, 44–45
Record label, 18–21, 25
Red Light Management, 19
Reframing your narrative, 30–31
Regulated capitalism, 6, 66, 89
REM, 18
Resetting your destination, 65–80
     foundational myths when, 74–77
     as a process, 77–78
     and sense of becoming, 78–79
     steps to, 71–74
     using personal values to, 69–71
Respect, 71
Results, delivering, 115–117
Revenue, as team goal, 130–131
Revenue Collective:
     in 2020, 158
     changes in, 159–160
     during COVID pandemic,
          155–158
     creation of, 2
     fee for, 96
     first hire at, 102–105
     growth of, 103–105, 123
     investors for, 209
     original goal for, 101
     scaling, 151
Rising Executives School, 193, 209–210

Robbins, Tony, 5, 189
Rolling Stones, 15
Roosevelt, Theodore, 128
Rosen, Jim, 69, 73, 78, 87, 106
Rue La La, 68
Running, 206

S

SaaS metrics, 151–152
Saint-Amand, Alexander, 13
Salary, base, 168
Sales, 21–22
Sales Hacker podcast, 103
Salesloft, 87, 89
Salespeople, role of, 129, 131
Sales Talent Agency, 162
Scaling, 125–131, 149
Scarcity mindset, 94
SDRDefenders, 210
Self-beliefs, 186, 205
Self-compassion, 191, 196, 205
Self-doubt, 186
Self-loathing, 188–191
Self-perception, 39
Self-pity, 27
Self-reflection, 69–71, 188–193
Self-talk, 190
Severance, 34–35, 173–174
Shame, 15, 16
Shaw, John Mark, 189, 191, 193, 199
Short-term thinking, 95
Silver Lake Partners, 66
Singer, Michael Alan, 205
60/40 relationships, 195
Skala, Emmanuelle, 65
Skok, David, 143
Slack, 123–124, 157
Smalley, Stuart, 190
Small people, 85
"Small short game," 33
Snowflake Computing, 141